Literacy
from A to Z:

Engaging Students in Reading, Writing, Speaking, & Listening

Barbara R. Blackburn

EYE ON EDUCATION
6 DEPOT WAY WEST, SUITE 106
LARCHMONT, NY 10538
(914) 833–0551
(914) 833–0761 fax
www.eyeoneducation.com

Library of Congress Cataloging-in-Publication Data

Blackburn, Barbara R., 1961-
Literacy from A to Z : engaging students in reading, writing, speaking, & listening / Barbara Blackburn.
     p. cm.
   ISBN 978-1-59667-078-5
1. Language arts—Activity programs. 2. Language
teachers—In-service training. I. Title.
LB1576.B495 2008
372.6′044—dc22

                                        2007051602

   10 9 8 7 6 5 4 3 2 1

Also Available from EYE ON EDUCATION

Study Guide
Literacy from A to Z
Barbara R. Blackburn

Classroom Motivation from A to Z:
How to Engage Your Students in Learning
Barbara R. Blackburn

Study Guide
Classroom Motivation from A to Z
Barbara R. Blackburn

Classroom Instruction from A to Z:
How to Promote Student Learning
Barbara R. Blackburn

Study Guide
Classroom Instruction from A to Z
Barbara R. Blackburn

Family Reading Night
Darcy Hutchins, Marsha Greenfeld and Joyce Epstein

Active Literacy Across the Curriculum:
Strategies for Reading, Writing, Speaking, and Listening
Heidi Hayes Jacobs

Building a Culture of Literacy Month-by-Month
Hilarie Davis

But I'm Not a Reading Teacher:
Strategies for Literacy Instruction in the Content Areas
Amy Benjamin

Literature Circles That Engage
Middle & High School Students
Victor J. Moeller and Marc V. Moeller

What Great Teachers Do Differently:
14 Things that Matter Most
Todd Whitaker

101 Answers for New Teachers and Their Mentors
Annette Breaux

Dedication

This book is dedicated to Fred, who provided me a new reminder of the inspiration and power of a teacher with vision, heart, and patience.

Meet the Author

Barbara R. Blackburn has taught early childhood, elementary, middle, and high school students and has served as an educational consultant for three publishing companies. She received her Ph.D. from the University of North Carolina at Greensboro. Now an Associate Professor, she received the 2006 award for Outstanding Junior Professor at Winthrop University, where she coordinates a graduate program for teachers, teaches graduate classes, supervises student teachers, and collaborates with area schools on special projects.

She has extensive experience working with K-12 teachers providing staff development in the areas of motivation, instructional strategies, literacy, working with at-risk students, and school reform. Barbara's workshops are lively, engaging, and filled with practical, relevant information.

If you are interested in contacting Barbara Blackburn, you can reach her at www.barbarablackburnonline.com or bcgroup@gmail.com.

Acknowledgements

To my family, whose support is always foundational to my success.

To my friends, who continually encourage me to focus on what is most important.

To Missy Miles, your feedback always makes my writing better. To Lindsay Yearta, your research support was invaluable. To Abbigail Armstrong, your insight is critical. Each of you inspires your students through your creativity and caring, and they benefit from your teaching.

To Dan Sickles of Eye On Education, this may have been your first book as an editor, but you provided key insights and guidance as we worked together. I hope I provided good practice!

To Catherine Thome, Pat Michael, Marie Verhaar, Colleen Politano, and Angela Fortune, thank you for your constructive feedback. Tackling a topic as large as literacy was a challenge, and you helped me make some tough decisions.

To Dave Strauss, I appreciate your creativity with the cover design. I love the rainbow!

To my colleagues at Winthrop University, who provide a collaborative working environment that allows me the flexibility to write and connect with teachers.

Finally, to the teachers in my life, my graduate students, those at Spaulding Middle School, the individuals who shared their stories with me, and all those who read my books and use the ideas to impact students, thank you. You make a difference every day in the lives of your students.

Topical Index

Literacy From A to Z is designed to support a variety of elements related to literacy in your classroom. You can progress through the book in alphabetical order, or because each chapter is like a mini-lesson, you may prefer to focus on chapters that address particular needs in your school and/or district. For your convenience, a topical index follows to assist you in your planning. This directs you to the main chapter(s) about literacy concerns, but keep in mind that topics are integrated throughout the book. For example, I specifically address comprehension in chapter H: Help Me Understand, but there are also comprehension strategies mixed into other chapters.

Issue	Recommended Chapters
Alternatives to Round Robin Reading	Chapters F, R
Assessment	Chapter K
Background Knowledge	Chapter C
Building Independent Readers and Writers	Chapter Y
Classroom Management	Chapters M, Z
Comprehension	Chapter H
Conferencing With Students	Chapter Q
Connections	Chapter C
Context Clues	Chapter R
Cooperative Learning	Chapter M
Differentiated Instruction	Chapter V
Displaying Student Work	Chapter Z
Fix It/Fix Up Strategies	Chapter T
Fluency	Chapter F
Grammar	Chapter P
Graphic Organizers	Chapters P, L

Table of Contents

Introduction

As the daughter of a teacher and a school secretary, I grew up knowing the importance of a teacher. I remember many of my teachers. More importantly, I recall the joy of learning I experienced with them. I can still tell you which teachers read to me and my classmates after lunch, which ones gave us opportunities to write creatively, and which ones challenged me to do my best rather than simply work for a grade.

When I became a teacher, I wanted my students to love language just as I did. Because of that, I wanted to teach students to read and write. My dream was to teach kindergarten or first grade, knowing I would see the shine in a child's eyes when he or she truly learned to read for the first time.

However, after a short time in elementary school, I was offered a position in a junior high school. Although that was a change, when I began teaching our remedial language arts classes I was able to use my skills to teach students who were struggling to read and write.

Some of my students came to my class carrying baggage, such as memories of past failures, negative comments from other students replaying in their minds, and even some less-than-positive experiences with teachers. As we worked together, however, they became more confident learners. They became better readers and writers. And I became a better teacher. I learned many lessons from my students, yet the three most important ones still resonate: a good teacher always makes a difference, great teachers do whatever it takes to help their students learn, and we must have a vision for our students that exceeds their current line of sight.

First, I don't know if you've ever felt this way, but after hearing everyone else tell me how to teach and seeing no visible signs of progress with my students, there were days I thought I didn't make a difference. Teaching is like planting a tree whose fruits may not grow for years. You invest lots of time, energy, and passion today, but you have to believe that the fruits of your labor will flourish sometime in the future. You do the work and you have to trust that there is a benefit in the future. It's important that every single day, you keep the faith. Your students watch you. They notice what you wear, what you say, and at times, even what you think! And every single day, every single moment, remember what Sam Myers, coordinator of an alternative school, says: "On your worst day, you are still someone's best hope." You are still their teacher. You, and you alone, are the key to someone learning today.

That statement is a powerful reminder of the worth of a teacher, but it's also a challenge. My second lesson was that as teachers we are called to do whatever it takes to help our students learn. That may mean investing extra time, attention, or effort to determine what to do when nothing is working. My focus in this book is to provide a toolbox of sorts, filled with a variety of activities and strategies that can help. Your job, of course, is to determine which ones work best with each of your students.

Finally, probably the most powerful lesson I learned from my students was the importance of my vision. I needed to see them as more than who they were at that moment. I think that's because, without a vision, the first two points lose some power.

Just as butterflies are not in their final beautiful state when they are born, or when they are caterpillars, or when they form into a chrysalis, so our students are not in their final beautiful state when we are teaching them. Think about that for a minute. Where are the students you teach? Are they newborn? Are they caterpillars? Or are they inside a chrysalis? What does that mean to you? If you think about your students as *butterflies in the making,* how does that change how you view them? One of the most difficult things for teachers to do is to keep our expectations high, especially when our students' actions make us think less of them. There were days my students challenged me to come up with any positive thoughts about them, but those were the days they needed me the most. I found they needed me to believe they are butterflies when they were most acting like worms!

This book does not provide you with a rigid program of step-by-step instructions. Rather, it is a set of recommended actions that, when persistently and consistently applied, help your students become better readers, writers, speakers, listeners, and thinkers! As you read, you'll find 26 chapters, one for each letter of the alphabet. The chapters are not sequential; they are designed so you can start with any area that interests you or that meets a current need. I have provided a topical index (see pages ix–x) for your reference. It's also important to understand that this is just a synopsis of key topics in literacy instruction. As I wrote, there were many times I thought, "Wow! I could write another chapter on that topic," but there are only 26 letters of the alphabet, so I chose ones that provide an overview.

Throughout the chapters, you will find stories from my classroom and from classrooms of other literacy teachers. The stories serve as lampposts, guiding you to new directions for your classroom. At times, you'll hear the voices of students whose names have been changed to protect their privacy in most cases.

As I travel across the nation, I am saddened as I listen to teachers share their feelings of discouragement. As you read, you'll find a common thread through every chapter. You do make a difference and your students need you to make a difference for them. It is my hope that you connect with your students in new ways as you apply the strategies in each chapter, and that you also feel a sense of renewal. Envision an adventure of literacy and enjoy the journey!

FYI

Electronic versions of selected figures and tables from this book are available at http://www.barbarablackburnonline.com

---

A

Answering Big Questions

It is better to know some of the questions than all of the answers.

James Thurber

Think About It

What is your biggest challenge as a literacy teacher?

As I work with teachers, they often ask me questions about their challenges and frustrations. I find those issues reflect the ones I faced. My struggles revolved around four major questions.

Four Questions

1. What is the best way to teach literacy?
2. How can I motivate my students?
3. How should I deal with standardized testing?
4. How can I be a creative teacher?

What Is the Best Way to Teach Literacy?

There are so many methods, recommendations, and programs for teaching literacy. Which one is right? My view is simple. There is no one correct approach that is perfect for every student. But we do know there are some general principles that make a difference with all students:

- Students need to read and write regularly and see literacy as an integral part of learning.
- Students need to experience language regularly, authentically, and in a variety of ways.
- Students need instruction in literacy. They become better readers and writers when supported by instruction that teaches them how to grow and improve.

I've found that within those general parameters, there is some wiggle room. For example, some students need direct instruction in phonics, whereas others may not. The most important lesson for us as teachers is to remember that we need to learn about recommended research-based best practices, evaluate them in light of what we know about our specific students, implement the strategies that we believe will work, and monitor and adjust as we see how our students respond.

Instructional Cycle

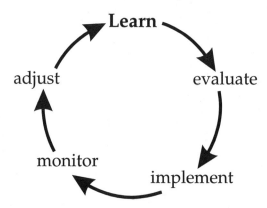

How Do I Motivate My Students?

If you've read *Classroom Motivation from A to Z*, you know that I believe all students are motivated, just not necessarily by the things we would like. Many of my students were not motivated by a desire to learn; they were motivated by the approval of their friends, the wish to earn some money, or something else in their lives. In our school, we had a basic system of rewards and consequences, so they would do what I asked. But, it seemed temporary.

That doesn't mean I never used praise or rewards, but I de-emphasized them. I learned that it was more important for them to be intrinsically motivated. My job was to create an environment in which they were likely to be motivated. People are motivated when they value what they are doing and when they believe they have a chance for success. Those are the two keys: value and success. Do students see value in your lesson, and do they believe they can be successful in your literacy classroom?

Value

Jill Mailler helps her students see value in poetry lessons through integration of contemporary music:

> It has been my experience that poetry is not something my students are interested in, whether reading or writing it. I now begin introducing poetry by having students bring in the lyrics to their favorite music. Using those lyrics, we discuss terms such as similes, metaphors, etc. By introducing poetry through the music students listen to every day they are excited to learn both the messages and how to write their own poetry (which usually is in the form of rap!).

Lindsay Yearta adds value through her choices of reading selections:

> My classroom library is chock full of a variety of books with characters from diverse cultural backgrounds. One of my African American students who hated to read at the beginning of the year wanted to read *Roll of Thunder, Hear My Cry*. The reading level was pretty difficult for her, so we agreed to read it together and discuss each chapter. After we finished that book, she asked me for a new book about every two weeks. I inquired about her sudden interest in reading and she told me that she now loved to read because I had given her books that are "like me." She had made it to fifth grade without encountering literature that reflected her culture.

Success

Helping students achieve success in your literacy classroom is the focus of the remaining chapters in this book. I discuss specific strategies to support their new learning and to scaffold their growth to increased levels. However, a first step is encouraging students to have a vision for success. One of my favorite ways to do this is to ask students to write vision letters. It's a simple assignment: Assume it is the last day of school. Write me a letter telling me why it was the best year ever! Evelyn Shuler's and Nancy Tindal's second graders show us that all students have dreams: "I learned how to read a chapter book." "I learned how to spell words like September." Vision letters help you tap into your students' goals and priorities, which you can then use to help them succeed.

Kendra Alston recently shared with me that she plans to have her students create Vision Boards. You can use poster paper, construction paper, or a file folder for them to write, draw, or paste pictures of things they want to be or do:

> They could add to it as often as they wish. Once they reach one of their goals, I would have them draw a circle around the goal/vision. I think this is a wonderful way for students to see their progress over time. In fact, for older students, I could ask the students to divide the board into four sections representing each academic quarter and ask them to do long- and short-term goals.

How Should I Deal with Standardized Testing?

The third major question I hear from teachers is more of a statement with a frustrating cry attached to it. "Standardized testing is taking over my classroom. What can I do?" During my fourth year of teaching, we began using a standardized test for promotion. I believe that we should help our students prepare for testing because it's simply not fair to test them on something they have not been taught. At a minimum, that means teaching the applicable learning standards, and making sure they understand the types of questions they will be asked. As much as I prefer essay questions, if the test is multiple choice, my students need to experience that prior to a high-stakes test.

However, a focus that is limited solely to a test limits you and your students. I believe that preparing students for a standardized, end-of-year test should be the floor, not the ceiling. In other words, start with ensuring that your students are ready for the test, but don't stop there. Abbigail Armstrong describes her view:

> My main goal is to teach my students how to do what they don't know how to do. It is not that standards and testing are not important, but I teach my students how to apply what they learn instead of just covering a new standard or objective.

How Can I Be a Creative Teacher?

Similarly, I am asked, "How can I be creative? I'm told what to teach, when to teach, and how to teach. Don't I have any choices anymore?" In an era of mandated standards, pacing guides, and even scripted lessons, this refrain is becoming louder. I was given standards and notebooks of test preparation lessons to use with my students. I found that I needed to balance those expectations with creative ways of meeting the needs of my classroom. Carie Hucks agrees, pointing out that as she sets up her classroom and plans lessons, she asks herself "What is best for my students first."

Connie Forrester, a former kindergarten teacher, describes her technique for being creative in her instruction:

> The best way to balance . . . is have a plan!!!!! With the age of accountability upon us, we must plan using the standards as the guide. Once you have designed the units of study, then you can be confident to teach using best practices and know you "will get it in." Textbooks should be a resource for all grade levels. Textbooks should never drive the curriculum, the standards should drive the curriculum and best practices are the vehicle to teach the standards.

In the end, I believe that good literacy instruction boils down to one thing: the teacher. The best program or textbook in the wrong teacher's hands won't make that much of a difference with a student, and a great teacher can instruct using almost anything! Throughout the remainder of this book, you'll read about strategies that worked for me with my students as well as those of other teachers. They are simply suggestions that, hopefully, you can use or adapt to help your students learn.

Summary

- Showing students the value of your lessons increases their motivation to learn.
- Success is difficult without first helping students create a vision or a set of goals for the near future.
- Preparation for standardized tests should only be a foundation for curriculum in your classroom. True education occurs when you require students to extend their knowledge by providing authentic opportunities for application of the standards.
- Be a creative teacher by thinking outside the textbooks; they should never drive your curriculum. Textbooks are only one small tool to help you teach objectives.
- Learning in the literacy classroom is not a linear process but rather cyclical in nature. One must always evaluate and adjust plans to meet individual needs.

If You Would Like More Information . . .

Engaging Young Readers: Promoting Achievement and Motivation edited by Linda Baker, Mariam Jean Dreher, and John T. Guthrie, The Guilford Press.

Literacy and Motivation: Reading Engagement in Individuals and Groups edited by Ludo Verhoeven, and Catherine E. Snow, Lawrence Erlbaum.

What Every Teacher Needs to Know About Assessment by Leslie Walker Wilson, Eye On Education.

This site contains the article, *Contexts for Engagement and Motivation in Reading* by John T. Guthrie: http://www.readingonline.org/articles/handbook/guthrie/index.html/.

This site contains an example of a language arts pacing guide: http://www.learnnc.org/glossary/pacing+guide/.

Classroom Motivation From A to Z, by Barbara R. Blackburn, Eye On Education (see Chapter I).

B

Building a Strong Base

He who has not laid his foundations may be able with great ability to lay them afterwards, but they will be laid with trouble to the architect and danger to the building.

Niccolo Machiavelli, *The Prince*

Think About It

What makes a difference with beginning readers and writers?

This chapter focuses on strategies to help beginning readers and writers build a foundation for the future. I've seen firsthand the joys of a youngster who says gleefully, "I can read!" And I've seen the frustration of one who can't seem to unlock the hidden codes of words. Helping each student be successful as they learn to read and write is one of our most important jobs.

First, there are five commonly recognized building blocks for reading.

Building Blocks for Early Success in Reading

1.	Phonemic Awareness
2.	Phonics
3.	Fluency
4.	Vocabulary
5.	Comprehension

I discuss fluency in Chapter F (Fluency Builds Confidence), vocabulary in chapter J (Jigsaw Puzzles), and comprehension in chapter H (Help Me Understand). Here, we'll look at ways to help your students with phonemic awareness and phonics.

Phonemic Awareness and Phonics

Phonemic awareness is simply being aware of the sounds that make up words. Phonics, however, is instruction that stresses the relationship between those sounds and the symbols, whether it is letters, letter families, or words. Both are critical beginning points for confident readers. If you teach prekindergarten, kindergarten, first, or even second grade, you are probably thinking, "I do this already. My reading instruction is all about sounds." And you are right. But, it's important to remember we teach sounds and the sound/print connection to help students make meaning. I was talking with a first grader the other day, and he told me that he is "supposed to know sounds. Sounds are the most important thing." My concern was that he could sound out words as he read a book to me, but he didn't comprehend any of the text. When you are teaching students to sound out letters and blend letters together to make words, the ultimate goal is to help students understand what they are reading.

Rhythms and Rhymes

One of the most effective ways to help students understand sounds and connect them to words is through rhyming. When I did my student teaching in a first grade, I chose books with predictable rhythms and rhymes, so my students could join with me as I read and reread the stories. This way, we learned sounds in context, reinforcing the meaning of words as well.

Predictable Books for Emerging Readers

- *If You Give a Mouse a Cookie* by Laura Numeroff
- *If You're Happy and You Know It* by Jane Cabrera
- *Teddy Bear, Teddy Bear: A Traditional Rhyme* by Timothy Bush
- *Here Is the Southwestern Desert* by Madeleine Dunphy
- *The Great Big Enormous Turnip* by Alexei Tolstoy
- *Have You Seen My Cat?* by Eric Carle

Rhyming games can also help students learn about sounds. One simple way is to have students match words that rhyme. I wrote the words on train cars, and they built a train of rhyming words. I was recently in a teacher's room where he adapted musical chairs to play Rhyming Chairs with his students. He would tell a story or say sentences with rhyming words, and students had to find a seat at a designated time (such as the second rhyming word). A teacher in one of my workshops explained that she plays Rhyming Ball. Students say a word, and toss a large beach ball. When the next student catches the ball, he or she says a word that rhymes, uses the word in a sentence, then says another word, and so on. Finally, to incorporate writing, you can play Fill In the Missing Word. After reading a story that is full of rhymes, write the sentences on the board or on sentence strips, leaving out the rhyming words. Students then fill in the correct words.

Creating a Print-Rich Environment

Another important way to help students learn to read and write is to make sure your classroom is filled with print. Label everything! I know I'm in an early childhood classroom when there are labels beginning in the hall, so that students are exposed to print even before they set foot in the classroom. Kendra Alston adds a twist to her labels, adding a descriptive word such as "crazy closet," or "wacky wall" so her students are more likely to remember the labels. As students entered her classroom, she asked them to "Read the Room." Every student decorated a fly swatter to create a pointer. Each morning, they went around the room, pointing at words with their wands and speaking the words aloud.

Pattie Thomas in Talladega, Alabama, shares a way to reinforce the alphabet with print. Each of her students creates an ABC book with environmental print: labels, pictures of signs, magazine and newspaper words, or whatever is a part of their world. I've played a similar game with my nephew Matthew. One night I call him and together, we decide on a letter. The next day, he looks for words that begin with that letter, so when I call at the end of the day, he tells me all the words he "found."

Beginning Writing

Although we could spend an entire chapter on beginning writing, I simply want to reinforce three key points. First, writing doesn't have to really be "writing." Writing is creating a story or list or set of directions in your head. Many of our youngest students write all the time, without using a pencil. When Jenna, my niece, was three years old, one of her favorite places was Super Wal-Mart. She would drag me to the lobster tank at the meat counter, where she would tell me stories about the lobsters. Of course they had names, and something exciting was always happening. That is emerging writing! Sometimes your students may draw a series of pictures to tell a story. And at times, they will write words, but they may have to translate for you to understand!

Second, I've found it's best to link reading and writing together. After we've read *Have You Seen My Cat?* by Eric Carle, I'll ask students how we can rewrite it. Perhaps we write *Have You Seen My Dog?* or *Have You Seen Our Teacher?* Creativity can run wild when students adapt one of their favorite stories.

Finally, I believe that beginning writing is about the story—not about handwriting, spelling, or grammar. There is a time and place for all that, but beginning writing is truly about the thought of creating something to tell someone else.

The Importance of Play

You can probably tell I believe in making learning fun. I have a less-than-pleasant memory of a teacher who drilled me with flash cards to learn letters and words. I'm not sure how much I learned, other than hating flash cards. Basic practice can help some students, but playing with sounds, letters, and words is more fun and helps students remember what they've learned. Connie Forrester describes the importance of play for emergent learners:

> Children are social by nature and play is one of the ways they make sense of their world and grow cognitively. You can almost see them go through Piaget's stages of learning as they play. Their play often resembles real life situations they have encountered and play allows them a forum to try out ideas freely. I think

it is important to realize that play occurs all over the classroom. I've noticed children in my classroom creating play scenarios that closely resemble mini-lessons they have encountered with me. Their mannerisms and statements to each other also show me they are using play to "practice" some new concept or idea they have encountered. Sometimes I overhear them working through complex ideas together. If children are immersed in an environment that is print rich and developmentally appropriate, then the pretend play becomes another vehicle for learning.

As you think about your classroom, how do you incorporate games? I'm biased—I think you can make almost anything fun if you want to. I asked Janelle Hicks to explain to me how she helps her kindergartners succeed as they move on to first grade. She replied:

> Magnetic letters, writing names, making names with clothespins and bottle tops, puzzle names, letter sorts, songs with letter sounds, alphabet charts, sight word books, alphabet puzzles, making letters out of playdough, tracing letters with fingers, writing letters and names with and on just about anything we can find to make it interesting!

For our early readers and writers, immersing them in an environment filled with sounds, letters, and words and providing intentional instruction to help them connect everything provides a firm foundation for their early success.

Summary

- The building blocks for early success in reading are phonemic awareness, phonics, fluency, vocabulary, and comprehension.
- We teach sounds so students can read words—and understand them!
- Rhyming games can help students learn about sounds.
- Creating a print-rich environment helps students put words with everyday objects.
- For early writing instruction, allow children time to play with words, sounds, and letters to make meaning on their own.

If You Would Like More Information . . .

Literacy Strategies: Resources for Beginning Teachers, 1–6 by Terry L. Norton and Betty Lou Land, Prentice Hall.

Phonics for Teachers: Self-Instruction, Methods, and Activities by J. Lloyd Eldredge, Pearson Education Inc.

Phonological Awareness: From Research to Practice (Challenges in Language and Literacy) by Gail T. Gillon, The Guilford Press.

Research-Based Reading Lessons for K–3 by Maureen McLaughlin and Leslie Fisher, Scholastic.

This site contains a lesson plan for building phonemic awareness: http://www.readwritethink.org/lessons/lesson_view. asp?id=120/.

C

Connecting the Dots

The ability to relate and to connect, sometimes in odd and yet striking fashion, lies at the very heart of any creative use of the mind, no matter in what field or discipline.

George J. Siedel

Think About It

How do your students connect new learning to what they already know?

I once heard a speaker say that connecting new and old knowledge allows students to find a shelf in their brain for the new information. Let's look at two important areas that can help your students connect the dots of learning: background knowledge and making connections.

Background Knowledge

Our students come in to our classes with a foundation of knowledge they already have about a topic. And some know much more than others. To effectively teach students something new, we need to know what they already know or think they know about a particular concept.

Although the most common way I see teachers discuss prior knowledge is through the use of a K-W-L chart, there are other alternatives.

K-W-L Chart

K (what I know or think I know)	W (what I want to know or learn)	L (what I learned after the lesson)

Missy Miles describes her K-W-L approach:

> As students come into class I hand each of them their own sticky note (which they love). I have a question or other directions written on the board that ask the students to tell me what they know about the topic we are beginning that day in class. For example, it may say, "List five things you already know." The students respond to the statement or question on their sticky notes and then place their notes on the board. After all students have responded, I read each of the sticky notes out loud, often times categorizing their responses into appropriate fields. By verbally acknowledging each sticky note, all students feel as though they have contributed to the "background knowledge board." More importantly, many students realize they know more about the topic than they first thought as they recognize other students' responses. I hear whispers in the class such as "Oh, yeah," or "I knew that!" It causes students to feel as though they can be successful at learning this subject because they already know something about it.

A more individualized and independent variation is to have students use a bookmark as they read. The bookmark is divided into three sections: before, during, and after. Before they read, they jot down what they know or think they know about the subject. As they read, they make notes about the text. You can choose to focus this, such as asking them to list the main idea from each section or describe the causes and effects of an event. After they finish, they write one or two things they want to know or want to learn more about.

Building Background Knowledge

At times, you may have a situation where students have minimal background knowledge. In that case, create an activity that allows them to build knowledge in class. Kendra Alston uses "Story Puzzles" to do exactly that. First, she asks students to skim a story and highlight several words they recognize. Next, they write the words on index cards and draw a corresponding picture. She explains that, through the cards, they are creating a puzzle of what they know. This accomplishes several purposes. They have an instant story starter; it helps them connect to vocabulary words as well as chunking the story; and most importantly, it helps each student build confidence in his or her own knowledge prior to reading. You can also buy blank puzzle pieces and make real puzzles out of their work!

Making Connections

Within lessons, students need to continue to understand how to connect what they are learning. There are three types of connections you can help students make: text to self, text to text, and text to world.

Text to Self

The first connection most students make is to themselves. As you read with them, and as they read independently, encourage them to tell how what they are reading connects to their individual lives. As students relate their own experiences to the characters and the story, their reading comprehension increases. There are several prompting questions you can use to discuss text to self connections.

Text to Self Connections Questions

- This reminds me of . . .
- I like (or don't like) . . .
- I know about . . .
- I feel (what emotion does the text prompt?). . .

Text to Text

Every time you introduce a new text to students, whether it is a book, article, or even a word, it's important to connect it to other texts they have read. I was in an elementary classroom where the teacher had a huge bulletin board at the front of the room. Students had drawn book covers for all books and other texts they had read. Whenever the class read a new book, the teacher posted a cover, and students used string to connect the new book with any other books that were related. The class created a visual web of connections for everyone to see.

I found I needed to encourage my students to think deeper about those connections. For example, if we read a fictional story, they only wanted to relate it to other stories. But I wanted them to also remember the news article we read on the same topic. Especially at the beginning of the year, it is important to provide more support and guiding questions to help your students make those connections.

Text-to-Text Connection Guide

Today's Story or Text:		
Connects to		
Other Stories or Books I've Read	Something in One of My Textbooks	A Newspaper, Magazine, or Internet Article

Text to World

Finally, you want your students to connect with the world around them. How does what they are reading link to something else they know or have heard about? Missy Miles incorporates text to world connections through readings of current events. Her fifth graders read news articles, and as a follow-up, make 2-minute oral presentations to the class. In addition to summarizing the event, they must explain how it affects them or someone they know. Students enjoy the activity, called "Keeping US Current!"

Teaching Connections

In her kindergarten classroom, Connie Forrester used hand motions to help her students remember the three types of connections.

Connections Motions

Text to text:	Hold your hands out like you are holding a book and move your hands from the left to the right.
Text to self:	Hold your hands like holding a book and then point to self.
Text to world:	Hold your hands out like a book and then raise both arms to signify the world.

She says, "I taught each type of connection separately using carefully selected read-alouds. After all three had been taught, then we made charts listing the different types of connections, who made them and what the connection was."

Sample Connections

Text to text:

    Three Billy Goats Gruff reminds me of Three Little Pigs because they both have three animals.

Text to self:

    Three Billy Goats Gruff makes me think of my name (Billy).

Text to world:

    We saw goats at Brattonsville.

Independent Connections

I've been in several classrooms where students were self-coding the connections they made as they read. Ideally, students can mark the text up with a highlighter, but that may not be practical. You could ask students to use a chart, or mini sticky notes (different colors for each type) to code the connections they make.

Connections Chart

My connections after reading _____		
T (text to other text)	S (text to myself)	W (text to my world)

Writing Connections

Don't assume that making connections is just about reading. Good writers make the same connections. In fact, as students focus on making these connections in reading, their writing also improves. Giving students an opportunity to think about their connections as they plan makes a difference. I think about plugging in a lamp. For it to light up, it needs to be connected. Your students' writings shine when they plug into their prior experiences and connect to a power source—themselves!

Summary

- We must know what knowledge our students already possess before we can begin to effectively teach them new information.
- When little to no background knowledge is present, it may be necessary to provide it for students in various ways.
- Within an activity, students must continue to make connections by relating the text to themselves, another text, or the world around them.
- Connections are also important in the writing process as students need to connect their prior experiences with new writing styles.

If You Would Like More Information . . .

Literacy for the 21st Century: Teaching Reading and Writing in Grades 4 Through 8 by Gail E. Tompkins, Pearson Education, Inc.

Strategies That Work: Teaching Comprehension for Understanding and Engagement by Stephanie Harvey and Anne Goudvis, Stenhouse Publishers.

This site contains lesson plans on connections: www.readwritethink. org/.

This site contains lesson plans on connections: http://www.reading lady.com/.

D

Designing Literacy Lessons

Setting a goal is not the main thing. It is deciding how you will go about achieving it and staying with that plan.

Tom Landry

Think About It

Does a lesson plan really matter? Or should you just follow the textbook or teacher's guide?

When I started teaching, my lesson plans were very brief. I remember one time I wrote, "Do pages 45–52." I wasn't completely sure how to plan; and as a beginning teacher, I was overwhelmed. It was easier to simply do what was written in the textbook. I learned that although a teacher's manual can be helpful, I needed to build my own plans for my students.

As you plan, you should ask yourself three simple questions.

Planning Questions

---

1. Why am I teaching this?
2. What do I really want my students to understand or be able to do?
3. How can I get there?

Why?

Notice the order of the questions. First, start with your purpose for that particular lesson: Why are you teaching that specific content? Is it foundational knowledge students need to understand to be successful in future lessons? Is the material something students will use in their own lives? During every lesson you teach, you should be able to answer the student who asks, "Why do I need to learn this?" And the answer needs to be relevant to the students, as opposed to "because I said so." You can enhance your students' motivation by helping them understand the purpose of the lesson.

What?

Next, turn your attention to the content of the lesson. What do you want your students to know or do? Is it "pages 22–24?" You have so much material to teach, what are the important parts? Some of the content in the textbook isn't necessary, and it's appropriate to skip those portions. But, you need to think about what is important so you can prioritize your teaching. Think about it this way: If I stood outside the door of your classroom and asked each of your students what they learned in your class, what would you want them to say?

How?

Once you know why something is important and what your students actually need to know, you can determine how to get there. A friend of mine says to make sure you are using the right tool for the job. You shouldn't use a hammer when you need to use a screwdriver or the job won't be completed correctly. Books, activities, and even your students' own writings are all examples of your tools.

Simple Plan

Lesson Focus/Standard(s)	
Why is this lesson important (purpose)?	
What is my goal (objectives)?	
How will we learn (lesson procedures)?	
How will we know we learned (assessment)?	

Planning for Follow-Up

Depending on your students and your style, you may want a plan that is more structured. This plan allows you to sketch out a whole group reading lesson, with follow-up mini-lessons for small groups based on specific areas of need. The mini-lessons can also be used as learning centers.

Whole Group/Mini-Lesson Planning

Lesson:	
Objective(s)/ Standard(s)	
Materials	
Procedures	

Small Group Focus Areas	
Words (examples: word sorts, chunking big words, prefixes and suffixes, analogies, context clues)	**Comprehension** (examples: recall details, sequencing, plot points, character analysis, comparing and contrasting)
Writing (examples: rewriting story with a different ending, rewriting story with different characters and/or setting, writing newspaper article about characters)	**Other** (examples: listening to audio of story for another purpose, choral reading for fluency)
Assessment(s)	

Writing Lessons

Multiple times during the year, I taught writing lessons that encompassed several days. In that case, I organized my lesson around the stages of the writing process.

Writing Lesson

Writing Activity/Focus:		
Standard(s):		
Materials:		

Day	Writing Stage	Activities
1	Prewriting/Getting Ready to Write	
2	Drafting/Writing First Draft	
3–4	Revision/Content Focus	
5	Editing/Grammar and Sentence Focus	
6	Publishing/Sharing Our Work	

Integrated Literacy Lesson Plans

Whether your focus is reading, writing, speaking, or listening, I believe a lesson is more effective when you integrate it with a text selection. Terry Norton, who teaches reading methods on our campus, uses a simple Before/During/After Reading Plan with his students. Lindsay Yearta points out, "The format helps me write a quality literacy lesson plan quickly and effectively. My students benefit from the thought process that I go through and the delivery of a quality lesson plan!"

Before/During/After Reading Lesson

Focus Area(s): ☐ Reading ☐ Writing ☐ Speaking ☐ Listening	
Standard(s)/Objective(s):	**Assessments:**

Literature/Text Used:	
Before Reading	
During Reading	
After Reading	

First, sketch out your objectives or goals. Align them with the appropriate standards. Then match those with assessments. When I was teaching, I needed to plan those pieces together. Otherwise, I might have a goal and get so caught up in how I was going to teach that I forgot the assessment! Then, consider what piece of literature or text to use in the lesson. This might be a children's book, a newspaper article, or your students' writings. At the same time, think about how you want reading incorporated in the lesson. Will you read to students? Will they read silently or to partners? Briefly describe that activity in the *during reading* section.

Now, let's back up. What do they need to do prior to that to be ready to read? How will you activate or build their prior knowledge (see Chapter C: Connecting the Dots)? How will you help them be ready for the activity? Do you need to preview the text? Or should you set a purpose for listening as they share their stories written in class the day before? Sketch that out in *before reading*.

Finally, go to *after reading*. What specific skills do you want them to apply? Perhaps you are working on sequencing. After reading a story with them, you want them to create a comic strip retelling of the story. Then, for a review game with a partner, they can cut the boxes apart and mix them up. The partner then puts them back in order. Or, you might ask them to write their own story following the format of the book. This links directly back to your objectives and assessments: What did you want them to learn? Now that they have read something, here is where they are applying that to show they understand the skill. And, after you finish, check off the appropriate literacy areas you've included. Your students will likely read, write, listen, and speak in almost every lesson!

Summary

- When designing a literacy lesson, first ask yourself three questions: Why are you teaching this concept? What should your students really understand at the end? How can you get them to this point?
- Students' motivation increases when they understand the purpose of your plan.
- Careful selection of the appropriate resources for your lesson ensures success.
- Plan intentional activities for each phase of reading (before, during, and after) to help students remain engaged from start to finish.
- Don't forget to plan for follow-up activities to reinforce new concepts.

If You Would Like More Information . . .

The Big Book of Reading Response Activities: Grades 4–6: Dozens of Engaging Activities, Graphic Organizers, and Other Reproducibles to Use Before, During, and After Reading by Michael Gravois, Scholastic: Teaching Resources.

Comprehension for Your K-6 Literacy Classroom: Thinking Before, During, and After Reading by Divonna M. Stebick and Joy M. Dain, Corwin Press.

This site contains links to graphic organizers, lessons, and writing prompts: http://www.manatee.k12.fl.us/sites/elementary/palmasola/writingindex.htm.

This site contains tools for reading, writing, and thinking: http://www.greece.k12.ny.us/instruction/ela/6–12/Tools/Index.htm.

E

Extra Support

Never look down on anybody unless you're helping them up.

Jesse Jackson

Think About It

How effectively do you meet the needs of your students with special needs and your second-language learners?

If you have a typical classroom, you teach students with a wide range of learning needs. Although one chapter cannot address all of them, I want to address two specific challenges: working with students for whom English is not their native language, and students diagnosed with special needs. As you read the strategies, you may notice similarities. Susanne Okey reminded me recently, "Although some strategies may work effectively with both groups, second-language learners do not have a disability. They simply have a language difference."

Students with Limited English Proficiency

Our classrooms are filled with students who do not speak English as their first language. Imagine how overwhelming that must be! While in an airport waiting for a flight, I was seated among people who spoke Spanish. I had some classes in Spanish in high school and college, but not enough for me to follow the animated conversation. I felt isolated and lost and was grateful that I didn't need any information from them. Our students feel the same way, but they need our information. Although this is just a starting point, there are two specific areas, verbal and visual, in which you can provide support for these students.

Verbal Support

First, don't assume that students don't want to talk to you simply because they don't speak the same language. Initiate individual, informal conversations that allow your students to connect with you. Also, speak naturally when giving instructions. Don't shout or speak too slowly; instead, break your comments into shorter sentences and speak at a normal (not fast-paced) rate. Finally, allow appropriate wait time for students to answer (at least 3 seconds). As a principal explained to me, extended wait time gives students time to process and transfer their thinking from their native language to English. Elke Schneider, one of my colleagues at Winthrop, suggests using choral response as often as possible for purposeful practice in saying the words. She also points out that it helps second-language learners repeat the correct pronunciation.

Visual Support

Next, because visual cues are particularly important to second-language learners, label objects throughout the room. A principal shared with me how she and her staff are adding a picture, a synonym, and an example for each word on their word walls to provide a scaffold for second-language learners as they develop language acquisition skills.

In addition to verbal directions, you can provide written directions for them to follow and concrete objects or symbols to demonstrate the concepts you are teaching. Using "realia," or the real object, assists ELL students build vocabulary. Although this is helpful for any student when introducing new information, it's particularly beneficial for students who can be overwhelmed with the sheer amount of new information they are exposed to. Elke suggests using visual cues for routine language arts assignments such as silent reading, journal writing, taking notes, buddy reading, and so forth.

Using visuals to support second-language learners doesn't have to be hard. Elke takes photos of stages students go through in tasks, enlarges and laminates the photos, and uses these as concrete reminders of the steps for standard tasks. One of my student teachers asked her second-language learners to help her teach vocabulary. She would go over the new terms and defiber the words. Kendra Alston offered an alternative to her students for journal writing: picture journals. For science journals, they drew the progression of an experiment, rather than writing a description of what happened. Utilizing movement is also effective. Dani Sullivan creates unique hand motions and body movements for each new vocabulary word. Her students retain the meanings far longer than if they simply read the definitions.

Students with Special Needs

It's also likely that you teach students with special needs. I speak with teachers all the time who feel ill-equipped to effectively teach these students. Although the issue is too complex for these few pages, let's look at several strategies that can help you.

Enhancing Literacy Learning for Students with Learning Disabilities

As Elke Schneider leads workshops with teachers, she provides several concrete strategies that can help students with learning disabilities learn successfully.

Strategies for Learning-Disabled Students

- Avoid teaching words that are the same or similar in pronunciation and spelling together because it sets these students up for failure from the start.
- Take the time to teach letter-sound patterns explicitly in a hands-on multisensory and carefully structured way.
- As prereading activities, engage students in hands-on activities such as sorting word cards by print patterns.
- Allow students to create a language folder that contains the explicit language support in a clearly structured one-page approach for the following:
  - Letter-sound patterns, their pronunciation, a key word, where they appear in a word, a context sentence and drawing
  - List of nonphonetic words that cannot be sounded out but occur frequently in content reading
  - Punctuation rules with illustrations
  - Color-coded sentence structure patterns with illustration
- Allow students to act out spelling, punctuation, sentence structure patterns, or word division rules to explicitly move their understanding from a concrete level to a more representational level (drawing what they acted out), down to the abstract level of just writing what they learned.

Using Individualized Education Plans with Special-Needs Students

Many of my graduate students share that one of their biggest challenges is the Individualized Education Plan (IEP) for a student. Unfortunately, many teachers don't know how to use that information and view an IEP as limiting or hindering their instruction. My colleague Susanne Okey, former special education teacher, has taught me that if you keep that information in front of you, and use it to guide you as you plan your instruction, it can be a powerful tool for the classroom teacher:

> Think of the IEP as a roadmap. It should be the result of a diagnostic workup that shows holes and significant gaps in learning. To integrate it all, you have to have IEP goals and objectives in front of you all the time. Put them in your plan book, not the file, so you see them every day with all other goals/objectives and

standards. Cover them as you are covering higher-level material or content with others, but don't eliminate higher-order thinking skills for this student.

For example, let's say that you are teaching how to write a three-paragraph essay. Sanchez's goal on his IEP is writing in complete sentences with appropriate capitalization and punctuation. How do you teach this when you are teaching others how to write an essay? On the other hand, you also want to start building the concept that writing is more than three short sentences. So, you might have him do a topic sentence for each paragraph. That might be the bulk of his essay, and he might work on that for period of weeks, but we don't want him to stay there. Let him participate in the discussion; he may be able to take it in but not produce it. He has a topic like everyone else, even though he may copy his topic from someone else.

Applying Lessons Learned: A Sample Activity

Mary Sanford teaches second-language learners and special-needs students at Sullivan Middle School. There are four key elements to her instruction for both groups: chunking instruction, cycles of repeated instruction, modeling for support, and use of visuals.

Teaching Characterization to Special-Needs Students and Second-Language Learners

My students lacked the vocabulary (for example, coldhearted, persistent, generous) necessary to describe characters and had limited exposure to working with characterization. I needed to break down the task and introduce it one piece at a time. I approached the task knowing I needed to model for my students. I modeled my strategies, I modeled my thinking, I modeled what I wanted them to do, and then we practiced, practiced, practiced.

Students were given a list of traits, both positive and negative. After reading the list together, students found words they would use to describe themselves. I modeled by describing things I do, and the students had to find the trait from the list that went with my behavior, such as, "I believed him when he said the dog ate his homework"—gullible. When they became comfortable using the list, they were asked to write down three of their own character traits and support why they chose each trait with an example of how they behave.

As we read several short stories, we discussed main characters and found words to describe them. We wrote paragraphs describing these characters using the new words we had learned. Using a Venn diagram, we compared two characters from the same story.

We were then ready to create our own character. I modeled this first by creating my own character by answering a series of guiding questions on the overhead for them to see. We discussed how the answers had to blend together for the character to be believable. Each character had to have a name and a problem they were dealing with. With this information complete, the skeleton "Fleshing Out The Character" from Janet Allen was filled in with what the character would do, say, plan, think, and feel [see chapter H: Help Me Understand]. We finished the project by illustrating the character. This hands-on component engaged every student. They could draw the character, but most chose to cut out body parts from magazines and put the parts together. This was fun and students had to know their character in order to put together a picture that matched their character's description and lifestyle. We put this completed work in a safe place and will return to it later in the year when we are ready to write a short story.

Mary also used picture books such as *Amazing Grace* and *I Wanna Iguana* to reinforce character traits. To extend learning, students read comic strips and had to "read between the lines in order to interpret the cartoon."

As you read the description of Mary's unit, you see how she plans a series of lessons in which she chunks her instruction into small, manageable bites. She then uses an ongoing cycle of providing instruction that teaches the same concept, but in different ways. Too often, we make the mistake of teaching the concept multiple times, but simply repeating the same lesson over and over isn't effective. She provides scaffolding through modeling and guided instruction and incorporates visual reinforcement throughout the lesson. The result? Both her second language learners and students with special needs are successful, confident learners. And isn't that what we want for every single student we teach?

Summary

- English language learners need a way to effectively communicate their ideas and questions. Visual and verbal cues are essential in helping them in the literacy classroom.
- Special needs students may need a variety of accommodations in the classroom setting, but it is important to still expose them to higher-order thinking skills.
- Hands-on, multisensory tasks benefit students with learning disabilities.
- The IEPs should not limit you; rather, they should be a guide as you plan your teaching.
- Chunking instruction into smaller, more manageable pieces helps provide extra support to students who need it.

If You Would Like More Information . . .

Comprehension Strategies for English Language Learners: 30 Research-Based Reading Strategies That Help Students Read, Understand, and Really Learn Content From Their Textbooks and other Nonfiction Materials by Margaret Bouchard, Scholastic.

Research-Based Strategies for English Language Learners: How to Reach Goals and Meet Standards, K–8 by Denise M. Rea and Sandra P. Mercuri, Heinemann.

Teaching Reading Comprehension to Students with Learning Difficulties by Janette K. Klingner, Sharon Vaughn, and Alison Boardman, The Guilford Press.

When English Language Learners Write: Connecting Research to Practice, K–8 by Katharine Davies Samway, Heinemann.

This site contains the article, *Reading Research and English Language Learners,* by Beth Antunez: http://www.readingrockets.org/article/342/.

This site contains information for parents and teachers about English Language Learners and is written in Spanish and English: http://www.colorincolorado.org/.

This site contains the article, *Teaching Writing to Students with LD* by Russell Gersten, Scott Baker, and Lana Edwards: http://www.reading rockets.org/article/215/.

This site contains strategies for teaching learning-disabled students: http://www.as.wvu.edu/~scidis/learning.html#sect5/.

This site contains articles, information, and recommended resources for teaching reading to learning-disabled students: http://www.ld online.org/indepth/reading/.

F

Fluency Builds Confidence

Confidence is the hinge on the door to success.

Mary O'Hare Dumas

Think About It

Do you teach a student who lacks confidence in his or her reading ability?

This chapter became very personal to me when my nephew began first grade. Matthew is phenomenal in so many ways, and of course I'm totally biased about his abilities. However, a few weeks into first grade, I received a phone call from my sister. It seems that Matthew was struggling to recognize words, which was negatively affecting his confidence and desire. Given a choice, Matthew would probably go outside and play, but we'd read enough books together that I knew something wasn't right. He was a better reader than I was hearing described. A combination of structured tests about his new spelling words, the pressure of homework every night, and the stress level of the adults around him added up to a crisis.

My sister and the teacher worked together to create some interactive ways for him to learn and play with words. And my sister also focused on making reading fun at home. Several days later, Matthew called, excited to tell me he had read four books. My sister quickly qualified that "the books were easy ones." From my perspective, that didn't matter. Matthew felt successful because he could read the books. That is the point of fluency: to allow a student to read easily, flow through the story, and build confidence in himself or herself as a reader!

Fluency Does Make a Difference

In an age of higher and higher expectations, it would be easy to push students only to books that are challenging for them. And there is a place for students to experience more challenging text. But there is also the need for students to read familiar, easy text. In addition to building confidence, reading fluently is likely to be more enjoyable for students. This may increase their desire to read on their own. Fluent readers are also more likely to comprehend what they are reading because they are not focused on decoding individual words. In a literacy classroom, there are three elements that can support fluency: modeling through read-alouds, opportunities for practice, and self-selected text materials.

Modeling Through Read-Alouds

Students need to hear what fluent reading sounds like. When I was a child, my parents regularly read to me, as did my grandparents and other adults around me. But you probably teach some students who don't experience that. No matter what grade you teach, reading aloud to your students should be a regular part of your instruction. I read to my junior high school students, and they were mesmerized. On the rare days I forgot, they insisted I read to them. You are modeling for them what good reading sounds like; and for some of them, you are their only model.

I don't have a standard list of books you should read aloud. In my classroom, I tried to vary my choices, using a mix of stories, poetry, and even nonfiction. I have found that if you, as the teacher, enjoy reading something aloud, your students enjoy listening to you. Your enthusiasm is contagious.

Opportunities for Practice

A second element for building fluency is providing students with multiple opportunities to practice with and experience the text material. Kendra Alston began each day by sharing a poem with her elementary students. Students read the poem three times. "The first time, I read the poem to them.

Then, the whole group read the poem together. Finally, we read the poem aloud by small groups. For example, group four read stanza two."

She used choral reading in which the whole class reads together. Another effective option is echo reading, in which you read a phrase and your students echo it back to you, mimicking your voice tone and expression. A third choice is to have students read along with you, reading silently as you read aloud.

Reader's Theatre

Reader's Theatre is an excellent way to give students opportunities to read aloud fluently in smaller groups. By reading directly from simple scripts, students focus on the text rather than on trying to memorize their parts. Be sure to give them an opportunity to read the material in advance; if students read aloud the first time they encounter the text, they are more likely to focus on decoding words instead of comprehension. That is one advantage of Reader's Theatre. It allows students to practice with a purpose.

Student Activities for Reader's Theatre

Look over play.
Find and highlight your part.
Read the play three times.
Follow along with your finger.
Practice acting it out.

Adapted from Kenna Bartish, Second-Grade Teacher

Repeated Readings

Simply reading a book again and again is beneficial for building fluency. If you teach younger students and find the right book, you can probably read it again and again just for the joy of the story! I can call my niece Jenna and read *The Monster at the End of this Book,* and we never tire of it. At times though, you need to provide a purpose for rereading a book. This can also help you teach specific reading and writing skills. For example, you might read *The Very Busy Spider* by Eric Carle, multiple times, each time for a different purpose.

Purposes for Repeated Readings for *The Very Busy Spider*

Prediction:	What might happen next?
Sequence:	List each event that happens.
Sequence:	Act out the event/create a spider web with yarn.
Characters/Dialogue:	Act/sound out dialogue for each animal.
Writing:	Choose another animal and write your own story. *The Very Busy* _____.

Self-Selected Text Materials

As part of your classroom, build in opportunities for students to select books or other text materials for independent reading. I'm not saying you shouldn't ever assign a book to read, but students need some times when they can choose what they would like to read. Be sure that you have some materials that are easy to read (see Chapter U: Up or Down? for more information on leveled books) as a part of your classroom library. And, make it safe for your students to choose those materials. I visited a classroom where the teacher had all the lower-level books on a top shelf above her desk. If a student wanted one, he or she had to ask the teacher for it. The students who needed the easier books didn't have the confidence to ask for them, so the books were unused.

A Caution About Round-Robin Reading

When I visit classrooms, one of the most common activities I see is students reading aloud in class. The most traditional form of reading aloud is round-robin reading. You probably experienced this as a student; I certainly did. Everyone was assigned a short section to read, and we took turns reading our part from the story or textbook section. The first problem with this method is that each student is reading ahead to his or her section rather than listening to the student who is currently reading.

Recently, several teachers have told me they have solved that problem by shifting to popcorn reading. They randomly call on students to read, so students can't read ahead. Although that addresses one problem, it doesn't solve the major issue with reading aloud. The method requires students to perform without practicing. If you want to use this approach, you'll see better results if students read the text prior to oral reading.

Performing Without Practicing

Let me give you a personal example that I experienced recently. I was planning to sing "Happy Birthday" to a friend of mine. Although I am a self-confident adult, I know my limitations. I'm not a great singer, and my friend is. So I was nervous. I practiced for two weeks and still needed some reassurance and coaching from another friend before my performance. Then, as I prepared to sing, my stomach was filled with butterflies.

If you like to sing, you're probably laughing at me right now. But I have high standards for myself, and I don't like to stumble in front of other people. And, because I'm successful in some areas, I stress over something when I think I may not be successful.

Doesn't that sound exactly like some of your students? And I'm not talking about just your struggling readers. Often, your high achievers who are perfectionists have difficulty with this issue. When I'm put on the spot and asked to stand up and perform something, you simply aren't going to get my best work. And the stress of the situation outweighs most of the benefits. During oral reading, the focus on performance can undermine a student's fluency skills.

Many teachers use fluency probes, which are short (approximately one minute), timed readings of text. Using fluency probes has three benefits. First, they are an effective tool to help you assess your students' reading levels. Next, through regular use, students build their fluency skills. Finally, as a principal shared with me, they "help students celebrate their growth in fluency."

Fluency is an important part of your reading instruction. Creating an opportunity for your students to fully immerse themselves into reading a book confidently is one of the greatest gifts you can give them. Don't miss it!

Summary

- The point of fluency is to allow students to read easily, flow through the story, and build confidence in themselves as readers.
- Fluent readers are more likely to enjoy independent reading and comprehend what they read.
- Allow students to choose a book at their comfort and interest level sometimes rather than always making them choose a challenging text. This increases their confidence as they read fluently.
- Model fluency through read-alouds. Students of all ages benefit from hearing a great story read aloud.

- Activities such as choral reading, echo reading, and Reader's Theatre provide opportunities for students to practice fluent reading.
- When requiring students to read aloud in class, build in time for them to practice first, so their performance will be more fluent.

If You Would Like More Information . . .

Building Fluency: Lessons and Strategies for Reading Success by Wiley Belvins, Scholastic, Inc.

The Fluent Reader: Oral Reading Strategies for Building Word Recognition, Fluency, and Comprehension by Timothy V. Rasinski, Scholastic, Inc.

From Phonics to Fluency: Effective Teaching of Decoding and Reading Fluency in the Elementary School (2nd Edition) (Professional Development Guide Series) by Timothy V. Rasinski and Nancy D. Padak, Allyn & Bacon.

Partner Poems for Building Fluency: 25 Original Poems with Research-Based Lessons That Help Students Improve Their Fluency and Comprehension by Bobbi Katz, Scholastic Teaching Resources.

This site contains fluency lesson plans: http://www.texasreading.org/icare/lessons/fluency.asp/.

This site contains free Readers' Theatre scripts: http://www.aaronshep.com/.

This site provides a fluencymanual, including sample fluency probes: http://www.linkslearning.org/reading_links/readingmanuals/FLUENCYPARTICIPANT.PDF

This site contains information on fluency probes (scroll down): http://www.interventioncentral.org/htmdocs/interventions/cbmwarehouse.php

---

G

Give Me a Microphone

Conversation is food for the soul.

Mexican Proverb

Think About It

How do you incorporate talk in your lessons?

Oral literacy, a foundational activity in a literacy classroom, can take a variety of formats. It might include speaking in a formal presentation, participating in a drama, or Reader's Theatre. But at its most basic level, oral literacy is simply conversation with a clear focus: to give students an opportunity to make meaning or to demonstrate their own understanding. I explained to my students that classroom conversations were simply on-task talk, and because they were really good at talking, they would be great when we had our conversations. It helped me set a focus and then allowed me to build on their conversational skills to move into more public and performance types of speaking.

Helping your students develop their oral literacy skills does not have to be difficult. After my first book, *Classroom Motivation from A to Z,* was published, I asked teachers which ideas were their favorites. I was surprised to discover that the most popular response was one of the simplest ideas: give students a microphone. Erin Owens, a first-grade teacher, shared her story with me:

> My students share a great deal. I have found that a microphone has played a key role in motivating them to produce quality work. First of all, they love the microphone, at first they say it is like "being on American Idol." You can hear them more clearly and their voice is obviously amplified. This gains the attention of the audience more than traditional sharing. After the "glamour" wears off, they begin to realize that they are showcasing their work each time they "step up to the microphone." I began to see a MAJOR change in their motivation to produce the best work they were capable of to impress and entertain their peers.

Isn't that the point—helping our students do their best?

Katherine Ledford notes that by teaching students to talk, you are also teaching them to think critically:

> Students have to be able to talk through a situation to consider it completely. They have to be willing to listen, share, and respond to and with each other. . . . Students [have] to think critically by talking through a situation first, then responding to it by connecting to their personal experiences and exploring the outcomes through conversations with their peers and me.

Ongoing Opportunities

As you think about your own classroom, there are probably plenty of times that you can create options for your students to talk about learning. For example, I regularly visit classrooms where teachers use the Think-Pair-Share approach, asking students to think about an answer to a question, then pair up and share ideas. Or, they ask students to form small groups and discuss what they have read. One effective teaching tool is an Interactive Reading Guide, which balances independent student work with opportunities for discussion and oral reading.

Interactive Reading Guide

Hatchet

by Gary Paulsen

Chapter One

Together: Read chapter one in *Hatchet*.

Individually: Summarize the chapter in two sentences.

Together: Compare the summaries. Modify your summary if you choose to do so.

Partner A: Read the first three paragraphs aloud to your partner. Remember, use the right volume so that your partner hears you, but no one else does.

Partner B: Read the next three paragraphs aloud to your partner. Remember, use the right volume so that your partner hears you, but no one else does.

Individually: Make at least one connection on a sticky note (you may choose from text-to-text, text-to-self, and/or text-to-world).

Together: Share and discuss connections.

Together: Discuss the purpose of the hatchet that Brian's mom gave to him before he got on the plane. Do you think it may have other uses? Why do you think Gary Paulsen titled the book, *Hatchet*?

Individually: Write down an interesting and/or difficult word.

Together: Determine the meaning of the word using classroom resources. Reread the passage that contains the interesting and/or difficult word.

Individually: What do you think is going to happen next? Record your prediction in your reading log.

Together: Discuss your predictions.

Carie Hucks capitalizes on her middle school students' desire to socialize:

> I try to incorporate sharing into every lesson with my students. A trick I use is colored dice. I post questions specific to a lesson in the room and match the question with a number 1–6. I give each group of students a set of dice. They take turns rolling the dice and respond based on the number rolled. The novelty of being able to roll dice helps engage my students in the lesson more effectively than just giving them questions and asking them to discuss.

Another fairly standard activity that involves on-task talk is asking students to create their own questions. Students can work in pairs or small groups and make up questions about a story they have read, or to review for a test. Especially at the beginning of the year, I found that my students struggled with the open-ended nature of that activity. It seemed they needed a bit more support, so I made sets of question starter cards. They could draw a card and use the starter word or phrase to create their own questions. That extra bit of support was very helpful. Then, as the year progressed, they were able to craft high-level questions without any prompting from me or the cards.

Sample Question Starters

▪ Which character . . . ?	▪ How might . . . ?
▪ Why did . . . ?	▪ Where did . . . ?
▪ If . . . ?	▪ Which word or phrase . . . ?

Literature Circles

Amy Williams finds that literature circles are an effective option for student discussion. She points out that "each student has a role to complete and must use the tasks associated with the role to add to discussions of the book." That is important; otherwise, one student may dominate the conversation, while others simply sit back and listen. When I was teaching, I assigned specific roles to my students and rotated those roles regularly. I also taught them how to effectively communicate their roles through oral conversation prior to literature circle activities.

Sample Literature Circle Roles and Responsibilities

Discussion Director:	group leader, facilitates discussion; keeps an overall log of questions, answers, and unanswered questions
Character Collector:	identifies characters in story; asks questions about each character; logs information in character sketches
Plot Plotter:	identifies key points in the plot of the story; asks questions to clarify the plot and/or prediction questions about what happens next; develops a plot map of the story
Scene Sketcher:	focuses on the setting of a story; asks questions to ensure everyone understands all elements of the setting (location, time, context)

Grand Conversations

Connie Forrester describes one of her favorite kindergarten literacy activities, Grand Conversations:

> I would usually introduce this strategy in October during our unit of study on non-fiction. To introduce the strategy, I would ask the children if they knew what the word conversation meant. After some discussion, one child would usually come up with the fact that conversation is talking. I would go on to tell the children that Grand Conversations are one strategy that the big kids use when they talk about books. I would explain the ground rules to the children. You would be amazed how quickly the children catch on and how much they enjoy this strategy. They would beg to use it after we had read a book. However, I found Grand Conversations worked best when used after a non-fiction text.

Ground Rules for Grand Conversations

1. One person talks at a time

2. When you respond to a classmate, you make a comment, ask a question, or make a connection. Your response must match the previous person's train of thought. For example, if we were having a conversation about a spider's habitat and the next child began discussing what he had for dinner last night, the first child could pick someone else.

3. No one raises his or her hands. I explain to the children that when people have conversations no one raises their hands. We would either toss a beach ball to the person to talk or the child would sit up very straight to be recognized.

Understanding What *Good* Looks Like

I think one of our challenges as teachers is helping our students understand what we expect of them. As a first-year teacher, I didn't realize I needed to teach my students how to speak. After all, they talked constantly; why would I need to tell them how? But if we want students to grow in their oral literacy skills, we should teach them what to do, give them a variety of opportunities to practice, and allow them to assess themselves and each other. Lindsay Yearta and I collaborated on a simple rubric to help her elementary students understand her expectations for speaking in her class. This could also be done with your students as a way to help build ownership. She began by listing what she looks for as her students speak: whether or not they are on topic and speaking on levels that are appropriate for the audience or purpose, the level of their voices, and their confidence as speakers. We then created a simple criteria, using the acrostic SPEAK. Finally, we described what speakers look like when they are *not* doing *enough*, doing *too much*, or if they are *just right*. The complete rubric is on the next page.

Rubric for Speaking

	Not Enough ☹	Too Much ☹	Just Right ☺
S Stay on topic	We're not sure what you are talking about.	You're talking about so much; we can't pick out what is important.	We understand your topic and your most important points.
P Pick your volume	We can't hear you.	You don't need to shout!	Perfect volume: loud for whole group; soft for partner; medium for small group.
E Eye contact	You're looking down.	You're looking at everything but us!	You are looking at your audience throughout your talk.
A Audience	What you are saying is too easy for us; we know it already.	What you are saying is too hard; we don't understand.	Great! It's not too easy, and not too hard.
K Know your stuff	You look very nervous.	You're acting like a know-it-all.	We felt like you were talking with us and helping us understand.

Summary

- Oral communication is a foundational activity in a literacy classroom.
- Incorporate opportunities for oral communication within your daily lessons through strategies such as Think-Pair-Share, questions starters, or peer review.
- Literature circles can provide an excellent means of oral literacy in your classroom.

- Hold Grand Conversations so students can see what speaking looks like in a large group setting.
- Assess your students on speaking ability using a nonthreatening rubric to help them grow in the area of oral communication.
- Let students take the stage often in your classroom—give them the microphone!

If You Would Like More Information . . .

Read and Write It Out Loud! Guided Oral Literacy Strategies by Keith Polette, Allyn & Bacon.

Oral Language and Early Literacy in Preschool: Talking, Reading, and Writing by Kathleen A. Roskos, Patton O. Tabors, and Lisa A. Lenhart, International Reading Association.

This site contains a lesson plan centered on listening and speaking strategies: http://school.discoveryeducation.com/lessonplans/programs/listenSpeak/.

This site contains information on how to write readers' theatre scripts and contains access free scripts: http://www.stemnet.nf.ca/CITE/langrt.htm/.

Help Me Understand

A man thinks that by mouthing hard words he understands hard things.

Herman Melville

Think About It

When you ask students comprehension questions, do they respond with true understanding, or do they simply repeat words?

One of the foundational elements of literacy is comprehension. We all want our students to truly understand what we are teaching, whether in a reading, writing, speaking, or listening activity. I could write an entire book on comprehension strategies, but because I only have one chapter right now, I'm going to focus on activities in three general areas: general comprehension of text, sequencing, and digging deeper.

General Comprehension

Asking comprehension questions after students read or listen to a text is a standard activity in most classrooms. I found that it was important to vary how I asked students questions, so they perceived it more as a game rather than just a lesson. Students are typically more engaged when something is fun, and they also tend to remember the information longer. Sometimes I used story cubes (see pattern). I wrote different comprehension questions on each side of the cube, and students tossed the cubes to determine which question to answer.

Story Cube Pattern

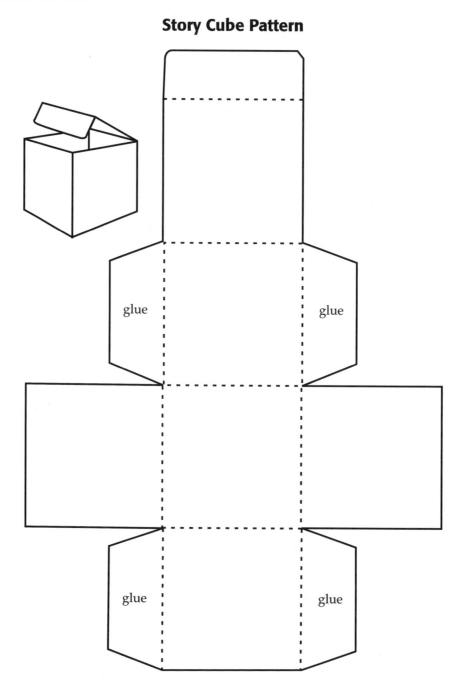

I also use a pizza wheel to review material students are assigned to read prior to or during class. Each student writes a fact he or she learned in one of the pizza slices. Then, working in small groups, students pass their papers to the next group member, who also writes a fact. This continues around the circle until each pizza is full. Students can discuss the material, using the pizza wheels as a prompt. Although you can measure students' understanding in an oral discussion, asking each student to write ensures that all students are involved in the lesson and provides an opportunity for every student to respond.

Pizza Wheel

Student: _____

Topic: _____

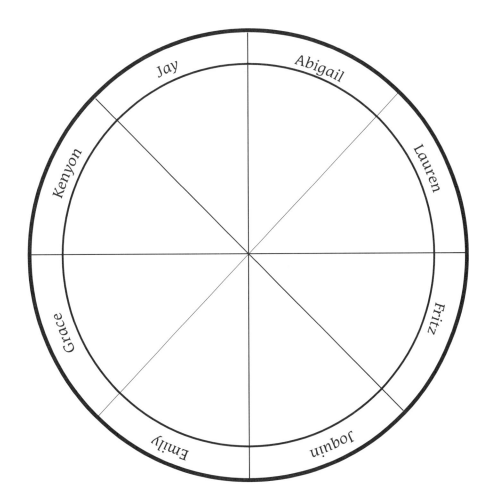

Kendra Alston focuses on comprehension elements through the use of Five Golden Lines. You can use any elements that match your lesson, just be sure that there are enough examples for the number. For example, because there is usually only one theme for a story, that always needs to go with the number one. Then, put the points on a PowerPoint presentation, or on posters, and count down with your students, giving them time to write the answers before you move on. It's an excellent activity to use after reading a story, or it can be used as a graphic organizer to help students plan a story of their own.

Five Golden Lines

5	Major plot points such as exposition, rising action, climax, falling action, resolution
4	Characters
3	Descriptive words about the setting
2	Examples of imagery from the story
1	Theme of the story

Connie Forrester adapted the elements for her primary age students as a countdown to help her students Blast Off for comprehension.

Blast Off

3	Connections (this reminds me of . . .)
2	Visualizations (this makes me see . . .)
1	Idea (this makes me think . . .)

Comprehension During Note Taking

You may also need to help your students understand content while they are taking notes. Kendra Alston uses a Guided Notes handout to help her students understand how to focus on key points during a lecture. As you can see from the sample on the next page, she provides a framework for her lecture on comprehension skills. Her students are able to easily follow her key points.

Guided Notes

Cause/Effect, Logical Order, and Compare and Contrast

Two _____ are related as _____ and
_____ if one brings about or _____
the other. The event that happens _____, is the
_____. The event that happens _____,
is the _____.

Cause/Effect Signal Words

Comparison

To point out what _____ or _____
things have in _____ is to make a _____.
Writers use _____ to make _____
and details _____ to readers.

Contrast

To _____ is to point out _____
between things. _____
_____
_____ _____

Similarly, she teaches her students to take notes while they are reading. This can be used during independent work, with partners, or in small groups. She and her students discuss the reactions you might have to text, and they create a coding system students use to mark text as they read. This encourages them to think about the content, but also their reaction to the text.

Marking System

X	I Thought Differently
+	New Information
!	Wow
??	I Don't Understand
∗	Very Important

Sequencing

Sequencing is another important part of comprehension. You can teach sequencing with almost any book that includes a series of events. One of my favorite books for young children is *The Bus Ride.* There is a clear sequence of events: A boy gets on the bus, then the bus goes fast. A girl gets on the bus, then the bus goes fast, and so on; the repetitive text makes it easy to do choral reading with your students. After reading the book aloud, I had my students act out the story, then we put character picture cards in order. I was in an elementary school classroom where the teacher had laminated posters of large train cars. During a second reading of a story, students posted sentence strips with each event listed on the train cars in the appropriate order.

Heather Harple, one of my graduate students, uses Chaining to teach sequencing. She gives students paper slips with different events from a story, and they reorder them appropriately. You can then have students copy the events in the correct order; or for a more interactive activity, you can have them actually chain them together, by linking the papers.

I also find it effective to teach sequencing through a prewriting activity called Storyboarding. To plan a story, I ask students to brainstorm ideas of different events that might occur, either drawing or writing each idea on a separate sticky note. Then, students can order and reorder the ideas by rearranging the sticky notes. I explained to my students that this is a simple version of Storyboarding, which is how Walt Disney planned his movies.

Digging Deeper

To encourage students to dig deeper than surface information, I used several questioning prompts and asked students to create their own questions about a text.

Question Starters

- What if . . .?
- How would it be different if . . .?
- Why couldn't . . .?
- If. . . . .then. . . .?

I was observing Jamie, one of my reading graduate students, and she encouraged students to create their own questions as they read a short story. They wrote their questions on craft sticks, and then played a game. If you prefer, you can give each student sticks in different colors so you know who created which question. Students drew a stick and answered the question. Because they created the questions, they had more ownership in the game and were more engaged.

In *Yellow Brick Roads,* Janet Allen describes an activity called Flesh It Out. Give students a picture of a skeleton and ask them to write different details about a character in a story, such as their thoughts (mind), their actions (feet), or words (mouth). I adapted the reading activity into a prewriting strategy when students are researching a historical figure. It helps students organize their thoughts, and it encourages them to move beyond standard information.

No matter what strategy you choose, helping students understand means giving them opportunities to show you what they know. And the more creative you are with your activities, the more engaged they are in learning.

Summary

- Students are more engaged and retain more information if you vary the way you ask comprehension questions. Make it fun!
- Use visuals when teaching sequencing to help students develop a clear picture of the chronological order of a story.
- Deepening comprehension strategies could include teaching the students to question the text or analyze character. Whatever you do to help students dig deeper, make it engaging!

If You Would Like More Information . . .

Action Strategies for Deepening Comprehension by Jeffrey D. Wilhelm, Scholastic Professional Books.

Improving Comprehension with Questioning the Author: A Fresh and Expanded View of a Powerful Approach by Isabel L. Beck and Margaret G. McKeown, Scholastic: Theory and Practice.

Reading Comprehension: Strategies for Independent Learners by C. Blachowicz and D. Ogle, The Guilford Press.

This site contains information on storyboarding: http://transitionstress manage.com/storyboarding.htm/.

I

I'm Stuck

Furious activity is no substitute for understanding.

H. H. Williams

Think About It

Do you teach a student who seems to spin his or her wheels? Or one who has given up?

In this chapter, we'll turn our focus to older students who, for a variety of reasons, are struggling with learning. And these may not just be students who are working below grade level. At times, even your brightest students can get stuck. Let me also caution you as you see your students in these examples. Learning is complex, and every student is unique. However, based on my experiences, there are some broad examples that can help us understand our students better.

For example, Marissa is a student with lots of potential—her fifth-grade teacher sees this and has identified several talents that are particularly strong. She is very creative, which comes out in her writing, on the rare occasions when she writes without worrying about what she is writing. Her major issue is that she doesn't trust her own judgment and opinion. In the initial stages of an assignment, she will pepper the teacher with questions. When she writes, her favorite time is the peer review, but rather than taking specific suggestions and implementing them, she continues to ask everyone for their opinions. She simply doesn't trust her own judgment.

What can you do as a teacher to help the Marissas in your class? Steve Siebold, a mental toughness consultant, compares the thought processes of the amateur performer and the professional performer. They are remarkably applicable to students such as Marissa. After all, what we ask students to do in learning is performance to them! We can adapt Steve's comparative categories to learning: amateurs are nonstrategic learners while professionals are strategic learners.

Nonstrategic Versus Strategic Learners

Nonstrategic (Amateur) Learners	Strategic (Professional) Learners
Doesn't think about thinking (no metacognition)	Thinks about thinking a lot, even without realizing it (metacognition)
Perspective of Self and Others	
Places high value on the opinions of others (needs constant reassurance)	Is confident of own decisions
External frame of reference	Internal locus of control
Asks for help first without trying to work out problem on own	Asks for help only after uses toolkit of own strategies
Connections	
Doesn't connect learning to other things unless made explicit by the teacher; doesn't realize that all connects to long term	Thinks about the what if, always making connections in head to self, other learning experiences, and future/real life
Cannot visualize an end product or a correct result of task or learning; doesn't know what it feels like to be right	Can visualize the end product or result of task or learning; is confident of correctness and/or being right

Nonstrategic (Amateur) Learners	Strategic (Professional) Learners
Views About Failure	
Views failure as the end, not as a learning process	Learns from failures; views failure as a learning process
Uses feedback and criticism as a stop sign	Uses feedback and criticism to improve
Problems and Solutions	
No plans for what to do if what they are told to do doesn't work	Plans for the unexpected and deals with those things; has alternate plans
Overwhelmed by problems	Deals with one problem at a time

Let's look at how these affect literacy learning.

Perspective of Self and Others

When working with students such as Marissa, begin by recognizing the real issue. She isn't simply bugging you, she truly doesn't trust in or believe in herself or her judgment. There is no short-term solution to changing beliefs, but there are actions you can take to support students like Marissa. First, when she comes to you for help, don't just give the answer. This may only encourage the dependency. Instead, guide her to the correct answer to teach her to problem solve. You may have to ask again, or wait, or reframe her words until you get a viable answer; but keep at it until she starts thinking about what she is asking. Provide encouragement when she attempts to figure it out independently first, even if she isn't right. Then provide more positive reinforcement for ultimately solving the problem herself.

You might also allow her to ask some other students for help, but with limitations. I have a rule, "Ask three before me," meaning a student should ask three students before they ask me a question, but it's limited to three. That may sound a little complicated, but it's like any other routine. If you take time to teach it to students, you save time later. Just count how many times students come to you for very basic, simple questions (What page did you say? Which problems? Where did you say to put this paper?)

Look for opportunities to positively reinforce her independent actions. Also, help her develop a list of the strategies she can use to solve problems. If your students keep a journal, have them designate a section and keep a log of strategies that have worked for them in the past. For example, if drawing a picture helps them remember a key concept, write that down so they remember it next time.

You might also choose to teach her a structured way of dealing with some common issues, such as encountering new vocabulary words. Some of my students had one response for figuring out the new word: Ask me! So I developed a simple set of procedures for what to do when they didn't know a new word. They quickly learned to try other options before they came to me.

What to Do When You Don't Know a Vocabulary Word

1. Try to figure it out on your own.

2. Read the sentence or look at pictures to try to understand what it means.

3. Check to see if the word is in the glossary or margin of the book.

4. Look it up in the dictionary.

5. Use a thesaurus.

6. Ask three other students for help.

7. If nothing else works, ask the teacher.

Connections

Nonstrategic learners don't even realize they are thinking, even when they are thinking negative thoughts. Marissa isn't connecting learning to herself or any other content unless you tell her. She feels like learning is a word search puzzle, with information hidden inside other letters, and she doesn't know where to look. To help her make connections, provide clear modeling of your thinking and use the strategies we discussed in Chapter C: Connecting the Dots.

Amateur learners also don't seem to make the connection between what you ask them to do and what that would look like if they are successful. I had one student turn in a book report; and in exasperation I said, "Were you even in the room when I explained this?" The reality was that Brian gave me what he thought I wanted, but he didn't understand. I've learned that the most important thing I can do to help my students with this issue is to show them multiple examples of what "good" looks like.

Views About Failure

A second difference between the strategic and nonstrategic learner is how students view failure. Some students expect to be perfect on the first try (and don't we all want that!). But when that doesn't happen, there are two choices. For struggling students, anything short of being right, which includes receiving feedback and/or constructive criticism, becomes a stop sign—a symbol of failure. For Marissa, the voice in her head says, "Because you missed it on the first try, you're a failure, so you might as well give up." This is compounded by the fact that Marissa had no plan of action if what she was told to do did not work. She tried to read the story and use pictures to help understand the story; but when that didn't work, she gave up. This contrasts with strategic learners, who use feedback and criticism to improve because they view failure as a learning process. They recognize that failure happens to everyone and that success comes from building off failures.

With my students, I openly discussed the role of failure in success by giving personal examples as appropriate to show that everybody fails. I'll never forget the night I brought my graduate students an article I wrote that had been rejected by an educational journal. They assumed I never experienced rejection, and it was helpful for them to see me respond to that in a positive way. We all have times that we are not successful, and it's important to show students how to overcome those times. Find reading selections about people who have overcome challenges to achieve and build lessons about these role models into your regular instruction. Also, encourage your students who do try, particularly if they are unsuccessful on the first attempt.

Famous People Who Overcame Challenges

Clay Aiken	Overcame issues with bullying during middle school to become runner-up on "American Idol"
Elizabeth Blackwell	America's first female physician, despite opposition from the medical community
Sally Ride	First American female astronaut
Grant Hill	Persevered to continue playing pro basketball after five traumatic left ankle injuries
Abraham Lincoln	Although from humble background and suffered several setbacks in his political career, became President of the United States
Wilma Rudolph	First American woman to win three gold medals after having been crippled by polio as a child
Henry Winkler	Famous television actor overcame problems with dyslexia and dedicated his life to being a role model for kids

Problems and Solutions

A related issue is that nonstrategic learners expect to do the same thing and get different results. The last time she had to do a project, Marissa waited until the last minute, didn't have the resources to complete it, and made an F. For the next project, she does the same thing. She doesn't see that working ahead of time and pulling together resources in advance will make the difference.

Strategic learners make plans for the unexpected. Playing *what if* allows them to deal with the unexpected. They also recognize that you must change what you do to get different results, which comes from a strong internal belief that they are responsible for results. To help your struggling students make the shift, plan with them. Before they begin a project, ask them to list several things they can do to be successful. Build the lists in small groups, and share the most important with everyone. Then, remind them throughout the project of the strategies, also giving them some suggestions of ways to deal with problems.

To counter the feelings of being overwhelmed, chunk your projects or activities. This can be as simple as listing out specific steps for completion on your board. You are really helping them write a to-do list, but it makes a difference. For long-term projects, require students to turn in pieces in smaller bites and highlight for everyone the specific step they should be working on.

Don't assume this is just for students who are working below grade level. I've seen these characteristics with some of my gifted students. They can struggle with a perfectionist approach to failure that keeps them from moving forward in learning. There is not a lock-step formula that works for each student, but realizing that their actions are based on beliefs about who they are and how they learn helps you adapt your instruction to support them.

Summary

- There are two types of learners in your classroom: those who are strategic and those who are not. Our job, as teachers, is to show all students how to become very strategic in the learning process.

- Encourage independent thinking in your students by providing encouragement, praise, and tools in which the students can begin to think on their own.

- Teach struggling students to make connections between the instructions you give and what the end result might look like.

- Students should be taught how to strategically use criticism and feedback as a springboard for improvement, rather than viewing any negative feedback as failure.

- Finally, to help students who seem stuck from the very beginning, show them how to plan for the unexpected in a given assignment and then chunk activities to make a seemingly overwhelming task much more manageable.

If You Would Like More Information . . .

Best Books for Kids Who (Think They) Hate to Read: 125 Books That Will Turn Any Child into a Lifelong Reader by Laura Backes, Prima Lifestyles.

Classroom Instruction that Works: Research-Based Strategies for Increasing Student Achievement (ASCD) by Robert J. Marzano, Debra J. Pickering, and Jane E. Pollock, Prentice Hall.

Helping Struggling Readers by Susan Fondrk and Cheryl Frasca, Good Year Books.

How to Reach and Teach ALL Students—Simplified by Elizabeth Breaux, Eye On Education.

The Struggling Reader: Interventions that Work by J. David Cooper, David J. Chard, and Nancy D. Kiger, Scholastic: Theory and Practice.

J

Jigsaw Puzzles

The limits of my language are the limits of my mind. All I know is what I have words for.

Ludwig Wittgenstein

Think About It

Do your students have a deep understanding of vocabulary, or do they simply memorize words?

For many students, encountering new words creates fear and confusion. When I was a student, the model for teaching vocabulary was predictable. We copied a list of words, accompanying definitions, and then wrote a sentence using each term. Finally, we took a test. The model is still used in many classrooms. That is like an upside-down V; a pointed introduction and the assumption that students will build a true understanding of the word.

Models for Teaching Vocabulary

Old Model   New Model

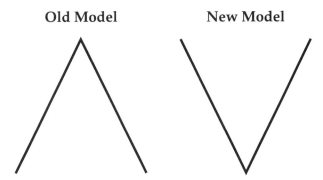

There is a more effective way to teach vocabulary: simply turn the V right-side up. Design your instruction to help students connect the new information with what they already know, give them a wide range of experiences with words used in a variety of ways, and provide opportunities to play with the words so they will leave your classroom with an understanding of the meaning of words.

Alphabet Books

Creating alphabet books can help you assess your students' current understanding of vocabulary. Beverly Simon asked fifth-grade students to list what they knew about math and what they wanted to know about math. Then she asked them to work together to create a math alphabet of terms. Through the process, she learned the broad concepts they knew, then she gained a deeper understanding of their true knowledge based on their existing math vocabulary.

You can also create alphabet books after a unit of instruction to determine how well your students understand what they learned. It's a fun, creative way to let your students show off their new vocabulary around a theme or topic. Although you can use this idea throughout the year, your students will also enjoy creating The ABCs of ____ Grade (insert your grade level) as a year-end wrap-up. Then you can use their book to start the year with your next group!

Vocabulary Prior to Reading

There may be times that you want to have your students work with vocabulary prior to reading a text selection. One way to do this is with Word

Sorts. After previewing the text, focusing especially on the topic, give students a set of words with which they are familiar. In small groups, ask them to discuss the words and group them based on whether or not they fit in with the topic. After reading the text, students revisit their word groupings and sort them again based on the reading. A more open-ended strategy is to preview the topic and have students generate related words on their own before reading the text.

Another approach is to have groups of students self-select words they want to learn. Prior to reading, students skim a short text selection and find three words of interest. Next, the group agrees on five words, then they focus in on those words during reading to determine the meaning. The game 3F: Find . . . Five . . . Focus mixes individual and group work to allow students to develop a deeper understanding of selected vocabulary within a passage.

Games for Vocabulary Instruction

Too often, we expect students to fully understand a word after they have read it one time. However, reading it multiple times doesn't necessarily ensure understanding. Playing with words in fun and different ways helps them learn. My students enjoyed crossword puzzles. Recently, I spoke with a teacher who does backward crossword puzzles with his students; the words are filled in and they have to write the clues. For his most advanced students, he asks them to create a puzzle that is a blend of the standard and the backwards version.

During Head Band, Erin Owens writes a word on a sentence strip and makes it into a headband. First graders in her class give clues to the person wearing the headband, who must guess the word. All students are involved, and the activity encourages her students to learn from each other.

Lynn Kelley prepares vocabulary word cards:

> Students get in a circle and the person holding the cardstock says the word and acts out one interpretation of the word. They then pass the cardstock to the next person who repeats the word. This person must either do a completely different interpretation or they may add to the previous interpretation of the word. They really go out on a limb and have no inhibitions when they do this activity. This also works particularly well for differentiating between homonyms such as *billed* and *build* or *sale* and *sail*. I break the class up into smaller groups and have several groups going simultaneously.

Bonnie Williams linked a craft project to her vocabulary instruction after a unit on Egypt. Students built paper pyramids, then used the sides and the base to write the term, a definition, a sentence, an example, and a diagram.

Poetry and Vocabulary

Another way to make vocabulary more memorable is to have students develop creative ways to help them remember the meaning of the word. Although they still need to understand the concept, giving them a creative way to show their understanding can be less threatening than a test or an essay. My students enjoyed creating Concrete Poems for new words and posting them helped everyone learn. We also used acrostics as memory tools, and as you can tell from this book, I still use them to help organize information in an easy format.

Concrete Poem

I spoke with a teacher who uses haiku, the Japanese patterned three-line poem, to review vocabulary. Prior to the test, her students work in small groups to create poems about the vocabulary words. Line one must include five syllables; line two, seven syllables; and line three, five syllables. It provides an interesting challenge to students to condense the information and present it following the pattern.

Personal Dictionaries

Many teachers require their students to keep personal dictionaries of specific vocabulary words. I've seen a wide range of options for this activity. Some teachers ask students to log all new vocabulary terms for each unit, others ask them to keep up with troublesome words, still others allow for students to choose the words they would like to include in their dictionaries. That is really up to you. What works best for your students in your specific situation?

In addition to notebooks or journals, I have seen two unique methods for organizing personal dictionaries. I was in a second-grade class where each student created word cards that hung from a coat hanger. The teacher had a word closet that was accessible to students. Later, I saw a fourth-grade teacher use folders with her students. Vocabulary words were written on small sticky notes so they could easily add new words or take out those they had mastered.

Bulletin Boards

A final way to enhance your vocabulary instruction is to use bulletin boards. I visited a middle school that was focusing on teaching prefixes and suffixes in language arts classes. Near the front of the building was a large bulletin board divided into four sections. Students brought in examples of words using the prefix or suffix of the week and posted it in the appropriate section. Not only did this provide a good review for students, it required them to look for connections to other subject areas.

Words Related to a Prefix or Suffix

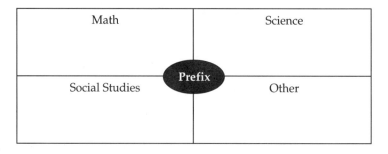

Similarly, you could do bulletin boards for other vocabulary activities. Examples include "Opposites Attract" for antonyms, "Train Station" for compound words, and "Figure It Out" for similes and metaphors.

Vocabulary instruction doesn't have to be a struggle for you and your students. Think of it as a journey. As you and your students explore the world of words, you'll find undiscovered treasures of knowledge. And isn't that more fun than simply memorizing definitions?

Summary

- Effective vocabulary instruction looks like a funnel. When you pour in connections to a new word, multiple experiences with a word, and opportunities for students to play with the word, the results are a true understanding of the meaning of that word.

- Alphabet books can help students express their understanding of key terms and ideas in your classroom—at any age.

- Selecting a small number of vocabulary words from a text and working with them prior to reading will help students when they encounter the word in context.

- Make vocabulary instruction enjoyable by creating various games with the words you want your students to learn. They'll absorb and retain information more successfully if it's not dry and boring.

- Find a way for students to keep track of their newly acquired words through a journal, a personal word bank, bulletin boards, and so forth so they can continue to see the word and recall its meaning.

If You Would Like More Information . . .

Stretching Students' Vocabulary: Best Practices for Building the Rich Vocabulary Students Need to Achieve in Reading, Writing, and the Content Areas by Karen Bromley, Scholastic: Teaching Resources.

Words, Words, Words: Teaching Vocabulary in Grades 4–12 by Janet Allen, Stenhouse Publishers.

This site contains vocabulary strategies: http://people.uncw.edu/sherrilld/edn356/notes/vocabulary_Strategies.htm/.

This site contains downloadable forms for vocabulary word maps: http://www.readingquest.org/strat/wordmap.html/.

Kids:
Learn, Watch, and Grow

If human beings are perceived as potentials rather than problems, as possessing strengths instead of weaknesses, as unlimited rather than dull and responsive, then they thrive and grow to their capabilities.

Bob Conklin

Think About It

When you watch your students, what do you see?

In this chapter we talk about an important concept: the use of ongoing assessment to design instruction. But that sounds really hard, so we're really going to discuss what happens when you look at your students to learn about them, watch their progress, and help them grow!

Learn

The first step is to learn about your students, but it's important to remember that growth for our students is never completely measured on a test. Susanne Okey, a former special education teacher agrees:

Achievement is supposed to be a benchmark of where students are so we can understand where they are learning and where they are in development. We measure infants in every checkup: Are their heads growing enough? Can we assume they are getting adequate nutrition? It's like that in schools; we measure whether or not they get adequate nourishment, are they benefiting from what we are providing or are we doing one size fits all model and leaving lots behind? We are in the business of nourishing children. We are nourishing their minds, bodies, and social development. Achievement often looks at the tunnel of academics only. This means we are not doing observation necessary to see if a child develops in all aspects. Then one day, you have a bright child who is doing well academically who falls off planet because no one noticed social problems.

For my students, I want to know about three things: their past, their present, and their future.

Past

I start by learning about where my students have been. As a teacher, you have access to test scores and other data about your students, but I'm a bit cautious about that. I have to be careful that I use that information to help me understand them, without prejudging them. That's a hard balance. As a teacher, I finally decided to wait until the end of the first month of school to look at their records. You must make that decision for yourself, but be careful that you learn from the information, and don't let it limit the student.

Kendra Alston asks her students to write autobiographies for her, with a twist. She has them write who they are and were as a reader, and then as a writer. She learns directly from her students how they view their learning and their progress, as well as seeing their perceived weaknesses. With younger students, interviewing them with similar, simplified questions will provide a wealth of information.

Writing Autobiography

Write your history as a writer. Think back to elementary school and describe what your teachers did to help you learn how to write. What have been your best writing experiences? What have been your most unsuccessful experiences? What subjects do you like to write about? What kinds of improvements would you like to see in your writing? What goals have you set for yourself in this course?

Answer the following questions in paragraphs, exploring each question as completely as you can:

- How do you get started writing?
- What is the ideal writing situation for you?
- Do you have any special habits when you write?
- How do you decide on the content and the form of your writing?
- Describe the process you go through, step by step, when you write. Why does this process work best for you?
- In what order do you make revisions?
- How do you know what to change when you are revising and what kind of revisions do you make most often?
- What writing problems do you have that need special attention?
- How do you decide that a writing piece is finished?
- What part of the writing process do you enjoy the most? Explain.

Note: This reflective assignment is focused freewriting. Think as you write. Put down as many examples as you can to illustrate your ideas. You may write in pen (blue or black ink) or you many compose at the computer.

Present

Next, collect as much data as possible about where each student is at this moment. If you organize your data collection to include both formal and informal assessments, you will have a great deal of information from multiple sources.

Sample Formal and Informal Assessments

Formal Assessments		
Name	**Brief Description**	**Helpful Web Site(s)**
State Standardized Assessments	These assessments are often administered at the end of the year and are used to assess growth in reading each year.	http://www.tea.state.tx.us/student.assessment/resources/release/ http://literacy.kent.edu/Oasis/Pubs/do-tests.htm
Informal Assessments		
Name	**Brief Description**	**Helpful Web Site(s)**
Reading Style Inventory (RSI)	The RSI assesses students' preferences and strengths in the area of reading.	http://www.avln.org/resources/standards/pdfs/iinventory.pdf http://www.educationworld.com/a_issues/chat/chat140.shtml
Teacher Observation	Teachers observe students to determine if the student has a physical weakness, is a reluctant reader, etc.	http://admin.loudoncounty.org/ourpages/departments/ESD-SED-Parents/english%20forms/observe%20forms%20and%20check/checkist_basic_reading.doc
Classroom Assessment of Reading Processes (CARP)	The CARP consists of grade-level stories that a student reads silently or orally. Following the story, the student answers a variety of questions. Teachers use the information to determine a reading level for the student.	http://www.pampetty.com/420iriadminister.htm http://lrs.ed.uiuc.edu/students/srutledg/iri.html

Informal Assessments		
Name	Brief Description	Helpful Web Site(s)
Cloze/Maze Informal Reading Inventories (IRI)	The cloze IRI is a set of leveled stories with missing words. The student must fill in the missing words. The maze IRI is very similar, with one exception. The Maze has a set of three choices for every blank. The students must choose one of the words to fill in the blank.	http://departments. weber.edu/teachall/ reading/inventories.html

The data can be confusing, particularly if you have conflicting information, such as a standardized test score for writing and the student's writing in your class. Perhaps a student's class work is excellent, but the test score was low. What do you do? Think of data analysis like a triangle. Those two pieces of information should be evaluated with a third data point: your teacher judgment.

Data Analysis

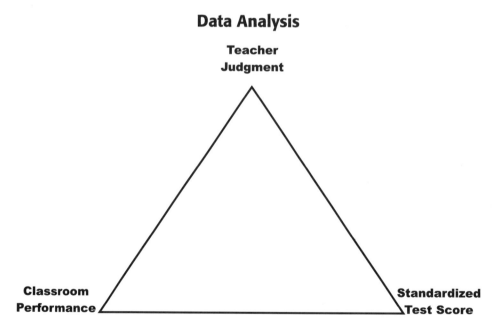

This is not a subjective, "Oh, I like Shane, so I'll ignore the test score." Using your judgment means that you factor in your observations and knowledge of the student to determine the validity of the data. Perhaps you've noticed that Shane thrives in your class and particularly enjoys writing. He has told you that he enjoys your class because you allow him to choose his writing topics. During the first parent conference, his father pointed out that Shane worries about whether he is smart enough to go to college, so he stresses over standardized tests. Your own evaluation of this information tells you that Shane's score on the state writing test is probably not reflective of his true ability. Again, data doesn't replace your judgment; it can help you make your decisions.

Future

If you want to help your students grow into the future, you must know what they think that future looks like. I mentioned in Chapter A: Answering Big Questions that you can learn about your students through vision letters. Ask your students to imagine it is the last day of school. Then, ask your students to write a letter explaining why this was the best year of their lives; it helps you learn about them. Chris Webb, one of my graduate students, opened his school year with the activity. "I wrote on the board for the kids to write why they had the most successful year in Mr. Webb's class. It was a great activity because I got to know my students early on, and I think the kids really appreciated starting off on the right foot."

Angie Krakeel and Kelly Zorn use vision posters with their students, which allow them to creatively express their dreams. Vision letters and posters help you tap into your students' goals and priorities, which you can then use in your instruction.

Watch

Once you have a picture of who your students are, the next step is to use this information to customize your instruction to help them grow. However, there's another critical part. You must watch their progress as they learn. I remember when my niece Jenna was 2 years old. If I took my eyes off her for even a second, she could get into trouble! That's true for your students during the learning process. If you don't watch them, they can go off in the wrong direction, which can lead to failure. So it's important to watch them during learning activities and document their strengths and weaknesses.

One simple way to do this is to keep a clipboard with index cards for each student. Then you can make notes as you monitor their learning. I kept a pad of sticky notes in my pocket and made notes on them. Then, after class, I stuck the notes inside individual student's file folders.

Connie Forrester explains how she adjusted her method of collecting information about her kindergarten students:

> I was gathering data on address labels. This method ensured that I gathered data from each child, because I could visually see which child's work had not been recorded. In February, I gave up that method of collecting data because there was not enough room to adequately record information and my observations. Then I moved to recording data on a blank sheet of paper to give me more room. This method worked well, but I could only see growth of the class at a glance, not growth of individual children. I finally moved to my present method of data collection, which is an individual booklet for each child.

You may prefer to use a form for multiple students. As a curriculum coach, Connie developed a simple way to assess learning and determine future actions based on that assessment. Patterned after Yetta Goodman's work, you'll see her chart for use with small groups on the next page.

Kid Watching

Week of: _____

Title of Book: _____

Level: _____ _____

Skill/Concept Focus: _____

	Notes	Reflections	Action Plan
Child One			
Child Two			
Child Three			
Child Four			
Child Five			
	This is where you record any observations from the lesson that are specifically related to your skill/concept focus for the lesson.	*This is where you record your thoughts on why the child made the errors. This could be phrased in question form. Example: The child repeatedly read a word using just the initial consonant. You record: "Is Child One using chunks as a strategy?"*	*This is where you record any ideas based on your reflections. Example: For Child One you could record: Play rhyming word game.*

Grow

As you collect and organize your information, you can use it to plan your instruction and help students grow to new levels. When I was teaching, I collected my data in a simple chart and coded the boxes with either a check plus (total mastery), check (mastery but review is needed), check minus (partial understanding), or minus (minimal or no understanding). That allowed me to scan to see individual student's needs as well as see students who needed to be grouped together for additional instruction.

Data Checklist

Student	Skill/Objective	Skill/Objective	Skill/Objective
Fred	✓+	✓+	✓+
Marisa	✓+	✓	✓
Julian	✓	✓−	✓−

Similarly, Kendra Alston color codes her observations of students: Green (Go Ahead), Yellow (Slow Down and Review), or Red (Stop for Much More Work).

Data are just sets of numbers unless you use them to make a difference in learning. Collect information about your students, and then watch them GROW:

GROW

G	Gauge where your students are.
R	Recognize their strengths and weaknesses.
O	One step at a time, provide instruction to help them grow.
W	Watch them rise to higher levels.

Summary

- Learning about your students includes an understanding of their past, present, and views for the future.
- It is important to collect data on a student from multiple sources to get a well-rounded picture of the whole child.
- Data should never replace your judgment; it should merely help you make decisions.
- Watch students carefully throughout the learning process to re-direct them when they get off course.
- Help students grow by using your knowledge of them, recognizing their strengths and opportunities for growth, and providing appropriate instruction.

If You Would Like More Information . . .

Focused Observations: How to Observe Children for Assessment and Curriculum Planning by Gaye Gronlund and Marlyn James, Redleaf Press.

Kidwatching: Documenting Children's Literacy Development by Gretchen Owocki and Yetta Goodman, Heinemann.

Learning to See: Assessment through Observation by Mary Jane Drummond, Teachers Pub Group Inc.

Using Observation in Early Childhood Education by Marian Marion, Prentice Hall.

L

Literacy
Across the Curriculum

Reading and writing are the wings that lift students to new levels of understanding.

Barbara R. Blackburn

Think About It

How do you use reading, writing, speaking, and listening to teach other subjects?

Literacy skills are foundational to instruction in all subject areas. I can't imagine any lesson that you might teach that doesn't include at least one component of literacy. Let's look at several easy and creative ways to use reading, writing, speaking, and listening to support lessons in math, science, and social studies.

Reading

Reading a section out of our social studies textbook or an article about a current event was a common activity in my classroom. However, if I asked students to read silently prior to a class discussion, they seemed to struggle and lack focus. I found it was important to give them a structure prior to reading. Sometimes I gave them an outline and key points to find. Other times, I was more open-ended with my directions. For example, I would ask them to read a section of their textbook and place at least three sticky notes throughout the selection. On each note, they can write a comment or a question about what they have read. The notes become the basis for our discussion in class. In addition, there are times I have them take the sticky notes out of the book, stick them on a piece of paper, add their name, and take it up for a grade.

Another option is to do a Scavenger Hunt and let your students work in groups to discover key points together. You are still simply asking questions for them to answer, but framing it as a Scavenger Hunt and allowing them to work together adds some fun to heighten your students' engagement.

Scavenger Hunt

Erosion Experiment

Science Activities A to Z by Joanne Matricardi and Jeanne McLarty

- Observe the sand in the table. Notice the large hill on one end. Feel the sand. Record what you feel and what you observe.

- Hypothesize: What do you think will happen to the hill when water is poured onto it?

- Locate the procedures. Write each step down. What is the importance of each step in the experiment?

- After you have performed the experiment, locate the vocabulary term, erosion. What is the meaning of erosion? How did the experiment demonstrate erosion?

- Find the expansion activity. What do you think would happen if you poured water onto a hill with grass on it? Make a hypothesis.

Several of my elementary math students who were quite confident working numerical problems struggled with word problems. The reading of the problem seemed to get in the way of the math! Teachers at Chestnut Oaks Middle School developed a graphic organizer to help their students break word problems into more manageable chunks. They systematically taught their students how to use the graphic organizer and provided multiple opportunities for practice. Picture codes were included to help students remember the steps easily.

Organizing Word Problems

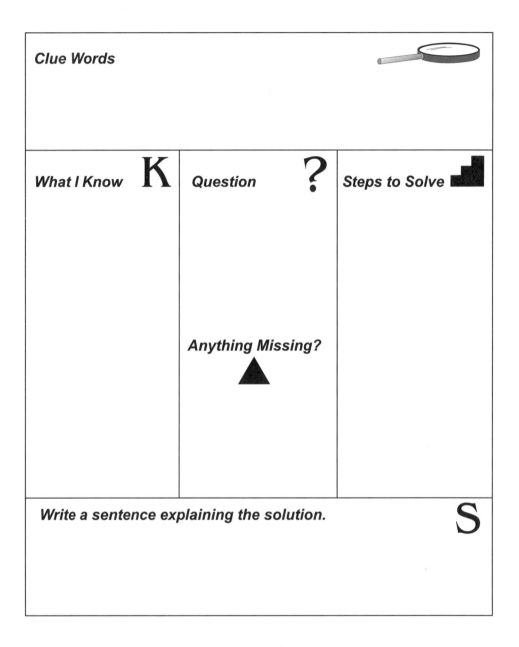

Clue Words

What I Know **K**

Question **?**

Steps to Solve

Anything Missing?

Write a sentence explaining the solution. **S**

Writing

For most of my students, note taking was a chore. They either wrote down everything I said, or nothing I said. I learned that many of my students did not know how to take notes, whether from my instruction or from a book. I began to teach them to use a simple note-taking format with two columns. On the left side, I provided an outline of the main topics I would teach. Students would then take notes about each point on the right. For more structure, I sometimes put the number of points they should have on the right side. I have seen teachers use a variety of other formats, but one of the most effective is a variation of what I used in my own classroom. It adds a third column for reminders, which allows students to come up with their own way to remember the content. This can be a picture or a word, anything that will jog their memory as to what the notes are about.

Three-Column Note-Taking Grid

Key Points/Topics	My Notes	My Reminder

Chris Triolo encourages his students to demonstrate their understanding of science concepts through the creation of a newspaper. As he explains in the assignment:

> You are the editor of *Plant Daily News* (or some newspaper of your choice). Your task is to design the front page of today's newspaper. As with a newspaper, the front page should be divided into sections. You should have each of the eight concepts we have learned in one or more of the sections. You must receive a score of 8–10 in order to have your article featured on the cover page. Be sure to follow the editor's suggestions.

He provides suggestions for columns, such as a weather feature, comics, sports, or business news, as well as specific guidelines for content.

Angie Wiggins uses poetry in her social studies classroom. When she teaches a unit about ancient Egypt, students read a myth about Osiris and Isis. After reading the myth, they write a biopoem about one of the Egyptian deities. The biopoem requires that students explain the feelings, fears, and desires of the god the student chose. After writing the poem, the students translate it into hieroglyphics.

Biopoem Form

God's Name

God of _____

Who feels _____(3 things)

Who fears _____(4 things)

Who would like to see _____

Resident of _____

God's Name

Sample Student Biopoem

Isis

Goddess of the dead

Who feels kindness toward everyone, love for her son, and happiness

Who fears Set, death of her or her family, and not finding Osiris's body

Who would like to see Egypt at peace

Resident of Egypt

Isis

Listening and Speaking

Natalie House reinforces listening and speaking through conversational activities in her math class:

> I strongly encourage my students to discuss mathematics. When they do, they internalize the concepts rather than my just telling them. Often, I will pose a problem and have the students work on it individually or in pairs. After they have had some time, I will have them discuss it with a partner. Then, I will bring the whole class together to discuss. I want students to feed off of each other and discuss without my being involved too much.

A Final Thought

Literacy across the curriculum is really just literacy. Ideally, reading, writing, speaking, and listening are such a natural part of your classroom that students expect to be doing those activities all the time. I've alluded to the importance of nonfiction and informational text in a literacy classroom. You may want to turn to Chapter W: Writing and Reading for Real Life, which gives you a variety of practical ideas that build on that concept.

Summary

- We are all literacy teachers—no matter what content area we teach.
- Reading content area text such as a social studies journal, science article, or word problem in math can be challenging. Front load your students with strategies for reading these informational texts to ensure maximum comprehension.
- Writing in content areas can be an equally daunting task. However, incorporating this aspect of literacy into these areas is crucial. Provide daily writing opportunities for your students!
- Allowing time for students to share their ideas and knowledge orally provides opportunities to develop strong speaking and listening skills.

If You Would Like More Information . . .

Active Literacy Across the Curriculum: Strategies for Reading, Writing, Speaking, and Listening by Heidi Hayes Jacobs, Eye On Education.

Literacy Across the Curriculum: Setting and Implementing Goals for Grades Six Through 12 by the Southern Regional Education Board (SREB).

Reading Aloud Across the Curriculum: How to Build Bridges in Language Arts, Math, Science, and Social Studies by Lester L. Laminack and Reba M. Wadsworth, Heinemann.

This site contains reading strategies for all content areas: http://www.pgcps.org/~elc/readingacross1.html/.

This site contains reading strategies for all content areas: http://www.mcps.k12.md.us/departments/isa/staff/abita/english/reading_strategies.htm/.

M

Managing the
Literacy Classroom

It is our American habit if we find the foundations of our educational structure unsatisfactory to add another story or wing. We find it easier to add a new study or course or kind of school than to recognize existing conditions so as to meet the need.

John Dewey

Think About It

What structures do you use to help your students be successful in your class?

I'm often asked about classroom management. How do you manage a classroom? From my perspective, management is not about having a set of structures and schedules; it's about having the procedures in place to help you meet the needs of all your students. Without a solid structural base, your classroom can become shaky, with unpredictable results for you and your students. Let's look at four key areas that can affect your literacy instruction.

Four Areas of Classroom Management

1. Student Participation
2. Routines
3. Clear Expectations
4. Small Group Activities

Student Participation

One of my struggles as a teacher was keeping all my students engaged, particularly during whole group discussions of a reading selection. It seemed that no matter what I did someone wasn't paying attention. I learned that I need to provide opportunities for interaction for every student whenever possible and that is difficult when I'm teaching everyone at one time. A simple but effective strategy is pair/share. Instead of asking a question about the text and calling on one student to answer, students turn to a partner and share their answers with each other. With this approach you know that everyone has participated, at least with his or her partner.

Brandi King points out the importance of calling on a variety of students during a whole group activity:

> Some students really don't mind sitting back while everyone else does the work. In return, some students don't mind giving everyone else the answers. My students now know that I will call on everyone regardless of who does or does not have their hand in the air, and I won't accept "I didn't get that one" for an answer. I make students think about a question before I pass them over to call on someone else. I also make them think about the answers they do give, by asking, "How do you know?"

Another challenge related to student participation is that of off-topic questions. I remember teaching a descriptive writing lesson, and my students were determined to ask me about everything else. I recommend having a parking lot: a section of your wall or board for off-topic questions. Students can write down their question on a sticky note and put it up on the parking lot. You can then go back and discuss it later when it doesn't interfere with your current lesson.

Routines

When students are learning, there are clear routines that provide a sense of stability and predictability in the midst of activity. It is a balancing act, providing enough variety to meet students' needs while adding enough structure and routine for them to feel a sense of control and predictability. Despite any protests to the contrary, students generally thrive when there is a clear system in place they can depend on and predict.

Connie Forrester describes the importance of routines for her kindergarten students:

> If there is one element that is crucial to the success of a teacher, then it is structures and schedules. Young children thrive on schedules and find security in knowing the routine. Routines and structures are equally as important as schedules, because without solid routines the schedule would not be as effective. At the beginning of each year, I would carefully walk the children through the day and tell my expectations of each segment. By having clear expectations, it also allowed the children to become risk takers and have ownership in the classroom.

I was reminded of the importance of routines when one of my graduate students e-mailed me in a panic. The tenor of her class had changed dramatically when the students returned from the Christmas break. I suggested she start with entrance slips. Students have 5 minutes to write down what they learned from the prior day's lesson and any homework. While this happens, she hands back the graded warm-up. Next, as they start on the new warm-up, she takes up entrance slips and determines how much she needs to review before she starts a new lesson.

By Friday, I received an e-mail update:

> My week ended so much better than it began!!! Entrance and exit slips are now permanent fixtures in my class. The kids have adjusted to them well. I decided to implement the slips in all of my classes and oh what a difference they have made. I also plan to start read-alouds daily . . . just for 5 minutes. I will begin with something that relates to some of the problems that my students may be experiencing now. I actually felt as though I was about to jump off of a cliff on Monday.

Both she and her students responded well to returning to the routine with some minor adjustments.

Sample Routines

Warm-up Wonders:	Warm-up activity is written on the board.
Be Still for Five:	Everyone is in their seats for first 5 minutes of class, silently reading, with no movement or leaving classroom.
Exit Slips:	Write down something you learned today and a question you still have; give it to teacher as ticket out of the door.

Clear Expectations

Clear expectations are also an important building block for the structure of your classroom. You probably have classroom policies, but they may be focused on discipline. I've found it's also important to have some that are related to your instruction. For example, my students knew if they asked me a definition for a word, my first response was, "Have you looked it up in the dictionary?" They quickly learned an unwritten rule of mine: Try it yourself before you ask me.

Natalie House has a more structured approach to the same issue:

> When students are working in groups, I give them question cards or question sticks. As the teacher, I decide how many questions they are allowed to ask during a particular assignment. I give the group that many cards or sticks, and take one each time they ask me a question. This helps the group depend upon each other and not turn to the teacher each time they get stuck.

Angie Krakeel and Kelly Zorn have a set of procedures as their sixth graders move from zone to zone (see Chapter Z: Zones of Literacy for more information on zones).

Policies and Procedures for Zones

- When we are in zones do not interrupt Mrs. Zorn or Ms. Krakeel.
- If you have questions:
  - First try to find the answer on your own. Read!!
  - Second find help from others in your zone.
  - Third write the question or problem down to be addressed by us during a transition time.
- Transitions should happen quickly. When time is up, time is up. You will have at least one other opportunity to complete the task that you are working on. Clean up your area and quietly move to your next zone.

As with most of my recommendations, I don't have a standard set of guidelines that are essential for you to use. Think about your students and your instruction and develop those expectations that support your teaching and help your students learn.

Small Group Activities

Group work is one of the most effective ways to help students learn. It can increase student motivation and is an important life skill. When I was teaching, some of my students didn't like to work in groups. They complained every day until I brought in a newspaper article that said the number one reason people were fired from their jobs was that they couldn't get along with their coworkers. That was an eye-opener for my students, but it was also a good reminder of the importance of working together.

In a literacy classroom, there are a variety of opportunities for students to work together: small group reading, choral reading, peer revision writing groups, Reader's Theatre, and so forth. However, group work is more effective when you create meaningful activities, design structures that ensure individual and group success, provide instruction to support the process, and make learning fun. Throughout this book, I've described many activities for students to learn together. As you try them in your classroom, help your students understand that each person has a role in the activity, and show them what being a good team player is like. Connie Forrester adapted a rubric from Missy Miles' fifth-grade classroom for younger students.

Student Cooperative Learning Rubric (Primary K–2)

	You're a Team Player 3	You're Working on It… 2	You're the Lone Ranger 1	Total for Each Category
G Group Dedication	I listened respectfully to my teammates' ideas and offered suggestions that helped my group.	I did listen to ideas, but I didn't give suggestions.	I was distracted and more interested in the other groups than my group.	**Group Dedication** I circled number 3 2 1
R Responsibility	I eagerly accepted responsibility with my group and tried to do my part to help everyone in my group.	I accepted responsibility within my group without arguing.	I quarreled and did not accept roles given by my group.	**Responsibility** I circled number 3 2 1
O Open Communication	I listened to others' ideas and tried to solve conflicts peacefully.	I listened to others' ideas, but did not try to solve conflicts.	I was controlling and argumentative to my group.	**Open Communication** I circled number 3 2 1
U Use of Work Time	I was involved and engaged; I encouraged my group the entire time we were working.	I tried my best the entire time we were working.	I was not involved and did not offer any suggestions for the good of the group.	**Use of Work Time** I circled number 3 2 1
P Participation	I was a team member. I offered ideas, suggestions, and help for my group.	I participated in the project, but did not offer to help anyone.	I did not participate because I was not interested.	**Participation** I circled number 3 2 1
				Total _____

For a sample rubric for older students, visit:
http://www.barbarablackburnonline.com/PDF/ClassroomInstruction/CooplearningRubric.pdf

Kendra Alston used color to help her manage her second graders' group activities. As her students worked through the various stages of the writing process, they wore visors to distinguish their current activity. Students who were brainstorming wore orange visors, those conferencing for revision wore green, and so on. At a glance, she was able to survey all students to see their progress.

Finally, Lindsay Yearta reminds us that it's important to be flexible with groupings, rather than forcing students to stay within a certain group at all times:

> I group the students who had a weakness in literal comprehension together. Groups are fluid and as students improve, they are rotated out of that group. As the year progresses, I am able to use my own assessments to determine what group to place students in. During writing workshop, if I notice that four of my students are not using commas correctly, I'll pull them during workshop time and work with those four on comma placement.

Summary

- Managing the literacy classroom is about having the procedures in place to help you meet the needs of all students.
- During group discussions, it is important to ensure that all students are actively engaged.
- Clear routines provide a sense of stability and predictability.
- Concrete expectations provide students structure and boundaries.
- Group work can be an effective structural component of the literacy classroom. It increases student motivation as well as comprehension when multiple students share various responses to a given text.

If You Would Like More Information . . .

Classroom Management Simplified by Elizabeth Breaux, Eye On Education.

REAL Teachers, REAL Challenges, REAL Solutions: 25 Ways to Handle the Challenges of the Classroom by Annette L. Breaux and Elizabeth Breaux, Eye On Education.

Time for Literacy Centers: How to Organize and Differentiate Instruction by Gretchen Owocki, Heinemann.

This site contains tips on how to manage a literate classroom: http://instech.tusd.k12.az.us/balancedlit/handbook/BLK5/bltablek-5.htm/.

Classroom Instruction from A to Z by Barbara R. Blackburn, Eye On Education (see Chapter W).

Navigating Research

Basic research is what I am doing when I don't know what I am doing.

Wernher von Braun

Think About It

When do you think students should start doing research?

Another important aspect of literacy is the ability to research a topic. When I mentioned research to my students, their eyes glazed over. They perceived it as something that was too hard and not useful in their lives.

Several years ago, I heard a speaker discussing the information overload in our information-rich society. He said that the amount of information available to us doubles every 24 hours and that the amount available would only increase in the future. With the Internet, e-mail, and other electronic databases the amount of available information is unbelievable. Learning how to find the information you need when you need it is the purpose of research, not some dry and dull paper on a useless topic.

Teaching students how to do research can begin early. Even primary age children can generate questions and look for answers. Those activities are the basics of research. Then, teachers can move students into more formal research assignments. Follow the same process you would with any type of new knowledge: build prior knowledge and help students set their own goals for learning, show them models of what a good finished product looks like, chunk the steps in the process, and provide multiple opportunities for feedback and revision.

I told my students that researching a topic was like being a detective. Lindsay Yearta uses the same analogy with her fifth graders. First, she provides a structured Detective Guide for them as they learn the basics of research.

Be the Detective!

Detectives always:

1. Get information from a reputable source!
   My information is from:

2. Document all information related to the source. Give credit where credit is due. If you use more than one source, list the others on the back of the guide.
   Title: _____
   Author: _____
   Publisher: _____
   Year published: _____
   Pages that I used: _____

3. Check information twice (Make sure you get the facts straight!).
   ☐ Checked it once
   ☐ Checked it twice

4. Take notes… write it down!

5. Put the information in your own words.

Then, as students mature in the research process, she transitions to a simple reminder bookmark.

Detective Bookmark

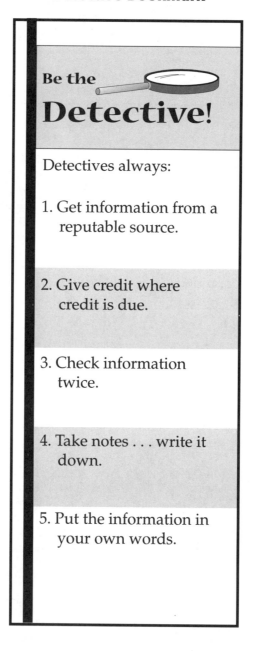

Be the **Detective!**

Detectives always:

1. Get information from a reputable source.

2. Give credit where credit is due.

3. Check information twice.

4. Take notes . . . write it down.

5. Put the information in your own words.

Research with Young Students

It's never too early to begin teaching students how to do research. Connie Forrester describes research projects for younger students:

> I had a menagerie of animals in my kindergarten room (tanks of goldfish and guppies; terrariums with worms, isopods, crickets, and lizards; a resident guinea pig; and an outdoor habitat designed to attract hummingbirds). Since I had arranged the curriculum into integrated units of study, it was simple to study each animal during the course of the year. As a culminating research project, I had the children complete a research project on the animal of their choice. I had 24 children and 8 different animals, so the children worked in groups of 3. Parent volunteers are a must for this project, so go ahead and line them up ahead of time.

Adding Creative Value to the Process

Tracie Clinton spices up the research process with her third graders:

> I give each of my students a person to research, a 2-liter bottle, a foam head, and two wiggly eyes. The students create the person they research with the items I provide. They add clothing and accessories. We also use class time to create individual PowerPoint presentations of their person. We invite parents and our principal to our classroom to view their projects that they work so hard on. The bottle people are also displayed in the media center for everyone to see.

When students research, write about, and present on topics, learning is enhanced.

Chad Maguire, a math teacher, asks his students to research and write about a famous mathematician. After giving students an overview of the project and sharing brief biographies of mathematicians, he randomly draws students' names, and then they hold a draft similar to a pro sports draft to select their subjects. The finished report must include standard information about the person, but students also present the information in a creative way, such as role-playing the mathematician or creating a game. As a final incentive, students earn bonus points based on the number of things they have in common with the person they research, which encourages them to move beyond basic information.

Missy Miles incorporates all areas of the language arts in her research activities:

> For biographies, my students dress like their person and give a speech about themselves. When we do colonial research, they write a historical fiction picture book to retell the story of the colony they research. We play "Will the Real Christopher Columbus Please Stand Up" and hold an "Ole Winfrey" show for Spanish conquistadors.

Reading, writing, speaking, and listening combine to help students bring research to life.

Research doesn't have to be difficult or boring. And it definitely should not be something that makes students feel like they are simply spinning their wheels, hoping to stumble on the right information. As teachers, it's our job to prepare them for the future. Research is a key that will help them unlock doors.

Summary

- A critical component in a literacy classroom is teaching students to find information they want, when they need it.
- Even primary age children can research by generating questions and finding answers.
- To teach the research process, follow the same procedures you would with any type of new knowledge: build prior knowledge, set goals, model, chunk steps, and provide opportunities for feedback and revision.
- Start simple, then progressively add complexity to the research process.
- Provide ways for research to be creative and exciting for students by altering the format of the research or the design of the end product.

If You Would Like More Information . . .

Exploring the U.S. on the Net: Internet Research for Elementary Students by Cynthia G. Adams, Good Year Books.

Exploring the World on the Net: Internet Research for Elementary Students by Cynthia G. Adams, Good Year Books.

Helping Students Write the Best Research Reports Ever: Easy Mini-Lessons, Strategies, and Creative Formats to Make Research Manageable and Fun by Lois Laase and Joan Clemmons, Scholastic.

Student Guide to Research in the Digital Age: How to Locate and Evaluate Information Sources by Leslie F. Stebbins, Libraries Unlimited.

This site contains lesson plans and information for the teacher about paraphrasing, Internet research, primary resources, and evaluation of sources: http://memory.loc.gov/learn/lessons/97/firsthand/main.html/.

This site contains a booklet for students to use with online research information: http://www.gecdsb.on.ca/d&g/ICT/Internet%20Guide.pdf/.

This site contains a format for students to use while documenting sources beginning in grade 1: http://nausetschools.org/research/works2.htm/.

O

Open Ears

A good listener is not only popular everywhere, but after a while he gets to know something.

Wilson Mizner

Think About It

How strong are your students' listening skills?

Whether you use lectures, discussions, small group instruction, or a blend of these activities, a basic element of success in the classroom is that your students listen. I learned early in my teaching career that my students didn't always know how to listen, so I needed to teach them how to be good listeners. I also needed to provide multiple opportunities for them to practice this foundational skill.

Teaching Students How to Listen

I found that I had to teach my students how to listen in my classroom. I'm sure they had been taught to before my class, but either it didn't connect with them or they forgot! Lindsay Yearta shared how she teaches her fifth graders. She created a simple acrostic bookmark to remind students how to listen. Then, she puts students in groups. "Each group is assigned a letter. They must determine how to act out that skill. For example, the 'L' group has to demonstrate 'looking at the speaker.' Then, students are handed the bookmark, which can be taped to the desk or laminated and given to the student to use anytime." You can use hers or create your own!

LISTEN Bookmark

Front   Back

Front bookmark with images for L, I, S, T, E, N

Back bookmark:

Look at the speaker

Illustrate in your mind

Stay focused

Tilt toward the speaker

Ears open

Nod your head if you understand or **N**udge me if you don't

Listening During Reading

One of the easiest ways to encourage listening is during read-alouds. Prior to reading the text, however, it's important to set a listening purpose. This doesn't need to be complicated; it can be as simple as saying, "While I read, I'd like you to listen for . . ." and give students one criteria.

Sample Purposes

- Types of words (nouns, adjectives, etc.)
- Words that start with a certain letter or sound
- Actions of a particular character
- Specific types of events

Listening to Each Other

Amy Williams regularly uses pair-share activities to encourage listening in her classroom. I've always found that to be a more effective way of increasing student engagement; it was hard for me to keep everyone involved in a large group discussion. By asking students to pair up and share their responses, you can increase participation and craft a strong listening opportunity at the same time. I use a variation of pair-share. After students talk with their partner, I lead a whole group discussion during which students can share answers. But rather than sharing their own answers, I ask them to share what their partner said. That sounds quite simple, but it raises the level of expectation for listening. As one teacher told me in a recent workshop, "If I had known you wanted me to share the other person's answer, I would have listened better!" That was exactly my point with my students. I wanted them to focus on truly listening. Asking them to share their partner's answer rather than their own encourages them to do so.

Listening to Provide Feedback on Writing

Amy also uses Writing Response groups to encourage listening and speaking, which we discussed in Chapter G: Give Me A Microphone. "Students meet in small groups to read their current writing draft; group members offer feedback on writing and eventually, over time, the group discusses the writing rather than simply giving statements of advice."

Peer review and assessment groups for writing are another great way to encourage listening. As Amy points out, however, it takes time to move students into a real discussion, as opposed to simply stating what they like and think should be changed. My first year of teaching, I put my students into groups and asked them to listen to someone's writing and give feedback. They did not know what to do and most responses were "That's good," "I guess that's what she's looking for," or "I don't know what you need to do."

I learned to start by giving them some structured questions (see the chart below). Once they were comfortable with those, we created questions together as a class so they could see how to decide what to listen for. I always had some generic questions; but over time, my students became more confident and could listen and provide feedback. The critical lesson they learned was that they couldn't provide feedback if they didn't listen effectively.

Countdown for Listening

Descriptive Writing	Persuasive Writing
3 Words or phrases that paint a picture	3 Specific examples that support the author's position
2 Additional words or phrases that might fit	2 Arguments for the other position that should be considered
1 Question you have for the author	1 Question that is unanswered

A Final Idea

You probably take a moment at the beginning of a lesson to find out what your students already know about a topic. We know that activating prior knowledge is important. But Terry Norton, a colleague of mine, reminds us that it is just as important to take a moment to activate students' strategic prior knowledge: their knowledge of how to use the strategies necessary for learning during the lesson. So, even if I have taught students to listen, I still need to take a quick minute at the start of a lesson to say, "In this activity, we'll be doing a lot of listening. Who can tell me some things we need to do to listen?" With a couple of answers, you have everyone ready to listen . . . and learn!

Summary

- Teachers need to help students acquire effective listening skills.

- Appropriate body language and posture can improve one's ability to comprehend verbal information, but you must teach your students this strategy.

- Setting a purpose for a read-aloud allows students to listen for specific information.

- Raise your level of expectation for listening by including small group activities such as think-pair-share. Then, hold students accountable for communicating ideas shared by their peers.

- Listening cannot be mastered in one lesson; it is a learning strategy that takes much practice and review.

If You Would Like More Information . . .

Active Literacy Across the Curriculum: Strategies for Reading, Writing, Speaking, and Listening by Heidi Hayes Jacobs, Eye on Education.

Creating Competent Communicators: Activities for Teaching Speaking, Listening, and Media Literacy in K–6 Classrooms by The National Communication Association, Holcomb Hathaway Publishing.

This site contains listening rubrics: http://www.storyarts.org/class room/usestories/listenrubric.html/.

This site contains lesson plans for listening: http://www.okcareertech. org/cimc/downloads/Sample-Activities.pdf/.

Painting Pictures

All thought depends upon the image.

Ferdinand de Saussure

Think About It

When do students use visuals in your classroom?

Importance of Visuals

We live in a visual society. In fact, we are bombarded with images every day. I've found that our students can benefit from visual reinforcement during learning. When I began teaching, too often I relied solely on my words to paint pictures for students. But that is not enough. Visuals are such an integral part of our society that we need to do two things. First, we need to teach students how to interpret the visual representations around them. Second, we need to use visuals to support our instruction.

Interpreting Visual Representations

Think for a minute about the visuals you read or write in your life. I made a quick list, and it included diagrams, figures, maps, menus, labels, captions, charts, schedules, timelines, and graphs. Then I scanned through my house and office to find text materials that included something more than words and letters. I found magazines, newspapers, ads, food containers, manuals, cards, and catalogs. Then, there's what I can see on television and the Internet. We truly are surrounded by visuals, and it's important for our students to understand how to interpret what they see.

One of the lessons that surprised my students was on advertising. I showed them a range of magazine ads about smoking, and we discussed what they saw. Their initial responses revolved around how pretty, handsome, successful, and happy the people appeared to be. That led to a discussion of advertising techniques and propaganda. Students quickly realized that it's important to look beneath the surface to determine the real meaning of ads.

I was recently in Lynn Kelley's classroom, where she did a similar activity. After teaching types of propaganda, her students created videos demonstrating the various techniques. As she said, "I think they will remember it when they see a question on the state test because they had to create their own examples."

Using Visuals to Support Instruction

It's also important to integrate the use of visuals to help students learn. Let's look at two basic ways to incorporate visuals: using graphic organizers and using pictures.

Graphic Organizers

Using graphic organizers helps students visually organize information and encourages a deeper understanding of concepts. They can be used to teach almost any skill or concept, but we'll review several of the most common uses of visual organizers.

Venn Diagrams

One of the simplest and most effective graphic organizers I teach is the use of a Venn Diagram for comparison and contrast. But I begin by creating a physical Venn Diagram using two jump ropes on the floor. I pick a student to stand in one circle, then another one in the second circle. I ask students to guess what criteria I'm using to sort the students. I continue to ask students to stand in one circle or the other (or in the center overlap if the person fits in both categories) until they guess my criteria. I start with something simple, such as colors of clothing or type of shoes. Then I use characteristics that aren't as visual, such as common interests.

Next, I let my students continue the game, sorting people based on what they have learned about each other. Because I give bonus points for coming up with criteria that are different and harder to guess, the students look beneath the surface for more subtle commonalities. This serves as a concrete lesson in comparison and contrast, and students can build on it during reading and writing lessons.

Semantic Feature Analysis

For more in-depth comparisons, you can use a Semantic Feature Analysis chart. Simply build a chart to compare related concepts, and then set specific criteria for comparison. Let's say you want to help students make connections across texts (see Chapter C: Connecting the Dots). Rather than just asking them to compare the text, I can structure the chart to scaffold their learning. For example, if we've just completed an author study and have read multiple books by the same author, we can compare all the books for a further analysis of the author's style. A teacher recently told me she did this with several of Gary Paulsen's books, and her students were able to describe his style more effectively after the comparison. She also said one of her students commented, "Now I know why boys like his books more than girls!"

Simple Semantic Feature Analysis: Author Study

	Main Character in Story	Setting	Genre or Theme	Plot
Book				
Book				
Book				

Advanced Semantic Feature Analysis: Author Study

	Protagonist	Antagonist	Plot Characteristics	Literary Elements
Book				
Book				
Book				

Creating Timelines

At the beginning of one school year, I asked my students to create a timeline of their experiences. They included when they were born, years they were in certain grade levels, births of siblings, and other typical experiences. They also highlighted special experiences such as band camp, travel experiences, learning a new skill, and so on. Then, we created a class timeline, showcasing students' common occurrences.

With today's technology, I would now add photos by taking digital pictures. Through this activity, students are required to research information (to be sure their dates are correct), compile information, and then analyze and compare. As a bonus, you can a put the individual timelines in a notebook to create a class book, which is a terrific tool to help other students, parents, administrators, and substitute teachers learn about each student. It's also a great prewriting activity before students write an autobiographical essay.

Graphic organizers can be custom-designed to match your content, regardless of what you teach or the age level of your students. As you begin, teach students how to use the organizers. Model appropriate use, then shift responsibility to students (see Chapter S: See Me). You can also ask your students to create organizers for the information you are presenting. That process challenges them and also allows them to demonstrate that they understand the content. But remember that the purpose of a graphic organizer is to help students understand the material; it is not to demonstrate they can draw. Too often, we lose our focus when students spend too much time drawing the organizers. Although you may use a variety of organizers, limit the number. The focus in your classroom is simple: *learn the material, not the organizers.*

Using Visuals

To help her students understand the difference between what you can actually observe as compared to what you can infer from a picture, Donna Morrow asked her students to bring in photographs. Her students interpreted their photos and listed at least three observations and three inferences. Not only did they learn how to look at pictures differently, the lesson reinforced critical reading comprehension skills. It's also an effective prewriting activity to help students write a more thorough essay about a picture.

Recently, I visited two teachers, Darin Pearson and Angie Krakeel, who use "Image Grammar" (Noden, 1999) with their students. Angie describes the process:

> I use pictures or photographs and ask students to describe in their own words what is happening. After they share their words, I ask

students to pick out the verbs (actions) that are taking place in the picture. Then, I explain that a participle is a verb + ing, and students add "ing" to their verbs. Finally, I model a "painting with words" of what is occurring in the photograph. For example, "Twisting, turning, and shouting, the skier moves down the mountain."

You can customize your instruction by choosing different pictures. Because of the variety, you can review specific grammar skills without boring repetition. My students would have been much more receptive to this grammar lesson than a worksheet on participles, and I imagine they would have applied this knowledge to their own writing more effectively. Isn't that really the point of visuals? Use them to help your students learn and apply their knowledge in their own literacy lives.

Summary

- Visual images are a part of your students' lives. Help them understand and interpret the representations around them.
- Visuals can support your instruction. Graphic organizers help your students organize their thinking, which means increased learning!
- Pictures help students apply their learning to their own experiences. Students remember more when they can "see" it!

If You Would Like More Information . . .

Image Grammar by Harry R. Noden, Heinemann.

The Power of Visual Imagery: A Reading Comprehension Program for Students with Reading Difficulties by Karen P. Kelly, Peytral Publications.

Visualization: Using Mental Images to Strengthen Comprehension by Linda Zeigler and Jerry Johns, Kendall/Hunt Publishing Company.

This site contains a lesson plan for the introduction of the visualization strategy: http://www.readwritethink.org/ lessons/lesson_view.asp?id=229/.

This site contains visualization lessons and downloads: http://reading. ecb.org/teacher/visualizing/visual_lessonplans.html/.

Q

Quality Conferences

Teachers are those who use themselves as bridges, over which they invite their students to cross; then having facilitated their crossing, joyfully collapse, encouraging them to create bridges of their own.

Nikos Kazantzakis

Think About It

Do you enjoy conferencing with your students or is it something that just takes up your time?

One of my challenges as a teacher was conferencing with my students for reading and writing. I originally tried to hold regularly scheduled, individual conferences with every student, but I was quickly overwhelmed. Then I shifted to small group conferences, but it seemed like some students demanded all my attention and others sat without participating. Over time, I began to blend small group and individual conferences. I created a system that seemed to help my students, but I was never totally satisfied with our conferences. I learned that although it is important to want to conference with students, it's also critical to develop specific structures and strategies to help them be partners in the discussion.

Small Group Revision Conferences with Sticky Notes

Laura Belcher works with small groups of Oakdale Elementary School students to revise writing:

> During our writing workshop, I meet with a group of about five writers of varying abilities. Each student has a turn to read something they are currently working on (about a page of writing) while the rest of us listen and jot down comments on sticky notes. We write down what we think the student did well and what we noticed didn't quite sound right (it was repetitive, unorganized, confusing, etc.). Each student does about three sticky notes. Then we share our thoughts. It is interesting because most of us have similar comments. We give our sticky notes to the writer so he can use them to revise his writing. What is really interesting is that by the time the third person shares, he is noticing on his own what he needs to revise. The students really enjoy sharing their writing, and this allows them to do that in a more organized manner. I also feel that it is inspiring my lower students because they are hearing some incredible writing from my more prolific writers.

Managing Reading and Writing Conferences

It's a particular challenge to try to fit conferencing with students into a busy day. A teacher recently said to me, "I'm so frustrated! I can't possibly get to every student every day. What can I do?" Janelle Hicks provides a manageable approach to reading and writing conferences with first graders:

> During writing workshop and independent reading, I conference with one table every two days. That usually means that I get to two–three students a day. While we are conferencing, I just jot down a few notes about what they are doing and writing about that day and any problems I see. During Reading Workshop, I will take a quick running record about the book that they are reading and note if it is too hard, too easy, or "just right."

Running Record for Book Conferences

Date	Student	Book	H/E/JR*	Notes
*H = too hard; E = too easy; JR = just right				

Conferencing Guides

Lindsay Yearta developed a series of guides that can be used to help students take ownership of reading and writing conferences. In the first example that follows, students create a place mat for a nonfiction book. They bring the completed mat with them for a book conversation with the teacher.

Conversation Book Mat

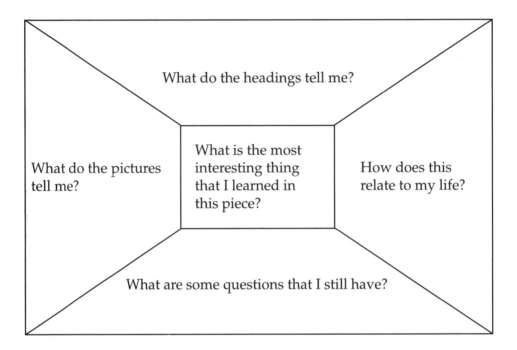

Lindsay also uses a Writing Bookmark (see sample on next page) for students to use in writing conferences. They use the bookmark to think about their writing prior to peer conferences and conferences with the teacher. Depending on the age of your students, you may want to adapt her questions.

Writing Bookmark

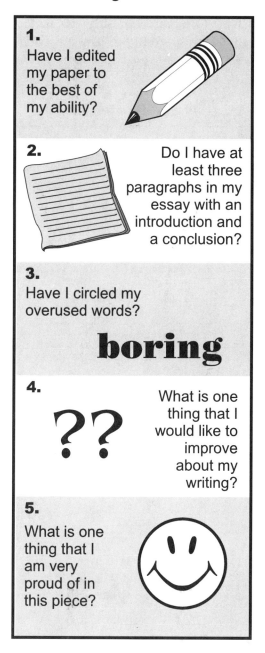

1. Have I edited my paper to the best of my ability?

2. Do I have at least three paragraphs in my essay with an introduction and a conclusion?

3. Have I circled my overused words?

boring

4. ?? What is one thing that I would like to improve about my writing?

5. What is one thing that I am very proud of in this piece?

A Positive Focus

Kendra Alston tries to inspire her students to love writing, so in her conferencing, she adds a positive flavor to their discussions. As she walks around her classroom, she stops to ask students to "think about what you mean. Now, let's write two good things you are doing as well as one wish."

Two Pluses and a Wish

Name	+	+	Wish	Score

When conferencing with individual students, she again focuses on growth. As she discusses writing with a student, they discuss ways the writing needs to grow, and ways it glows (Fletcher, 2006)!

Grows and Glows

Student Name _____

Conference Date _____

Grows

_____

_____

_____

_____

Glows!

_____

_____

_____

_____

After I saw these teachers effectively conferencing with students, I wished I could go back and try their ideas with my students. In each of their classrooms, they use reading and writing conferences to monitor their students' progress and help them improve their skills. And that's the key to effective conferencing.

Summary

- Develop specific structures and strategies to help students be partners in your conference.
- Although conferencing with every student each day may be impossible, you can set a more reasonable goal of reaching two to three students per day.
- Help students take ownership of the conference by having them come to the table with something to discuss.
- Highlight the positives when you conference with a student. By developing a love of reading and writing, students feel more confident.

If You Would Like More Information . . .

Conferences & Conversations: Listening to the Literate Classroom by Douglas Kaufman, Heinemann.

Easy-to-Manage Reading & Writing Conferences: Practical Ideas for Making Conferences Work by Laura Robb, Scholastic.

This site contains information on reading and writing workshops with discussion guides to aid the teacher or student in conducting a conference: http://www.bayvieweduc.ednet.ns.ca/Smoran/Reader'sworkshop/reader'sworkshopindex.htm/.

This site contains videos of a teacher holding writing conferences during writing workshop: http://quest.carnegiefoundation.org/~dpointer/jennifermyers/ workshopapproach.htm#/.

R

Recognizing Words

The popular education has been taxed with a want of truth and nature....We are students of words: we are shut up in schools, and colleges, and recitation-rooms, for ten or fifteen years, and come out at last with a bag of wind, a memory of words, and do not know a thing.

Ralph Waldo Emerson

Think About It

Do you teach students who can say words without understanding their true meaning?

Why do we need to teach students to recognize words? Because if they can quickly or even automatically recognize words, they can focus on comprehending what they read. Some students use phonetic clues to help them figure out words. Because we talked about sounds in Chapter B: Building a Strong Base, in this chapter we'll look at different ways to help students recognize words both through decoding and the use of context clues.

Looking for Clues

My students enjoyed being detectives and looking for clues, so I used that analogy with reading. I explained that if they came to a word they didn't know, there were several clues that could help them understand a word.

Types of Word Clues

- Word parts (prefixes, suffixes, word families)
- Pictures
- Sentence clues (synonyms, antonyms, explanations, and examples)

First, they could look for parts of the word they knew. This could be prefixes, suffixes, or even simply finding small words inside big words, such as houseboat. Next, there might be a picture in the text that would help. However, we also learned that pictures aren't always the best way to understand words. I made sure I taught a lesson on interpreting visuals (see Chapter P: Painting Pictures) early in the year. We spent most of our time learning how to look for clues in the sentence. I provided models of sentences that used synonyms, antonyms, explanations, and examples.

Sample Sentence Clues

Type	Example
Synonyms	Thankfully, the currency that England uses is easily exchangeable for United States currency so I would have plenty of money to spend.
Antonyms	The food at Betsy's house was plentiful, unlike the food at my house, which was nonexistent.
Explanation	Jonathon said that his school colors were crimson, a red hue, and gold.
Example	Deciduous trees, like maples, lose their leaves for part of the year.

You could easily expand this activity by putting your students in small groups and having them write their own examples of the different types of sentences. Groups can swap sentences and discuss the type of clue in each sentence. Then, throughout the year, as students read text and discover new words, they can use these clues to help them understand. I'd also recommend you have a *Detective Duty* wall or bulletin board where they can post words and examples of context clues.

Looking for Commonalities

Three Alike

Erin Owens, a first-grade teacher, uses a visual game to provide context for new words. During Three Alike, she writes three words on the board or overhead. Students then have to explain what the words have in common. This is a terrific way to help your class connect a new word to words they already know. You can categorize your words in a variety of ways depending on your purpose (parts of speech, common characteristics, beginning sounds, number of letters, etc.). As an extension, you can ask students to add other words to your list, or you can follow Lindsay Yearta's plan. She puts up several examples (at least six) and one nonexample. "The students have to determine which is the nonexample and what the rest of the words have in common. It's called the Red Herring Game."

Figure It Out

A teacher in a workshop told me she plays a puzzle game with her students, Figure It Out. She gives them a short paragraph or sentence, and they have to guess the activity and/or location based on the context clues. Students also underline specific words or phrases and explain how the phrase helped them know the location or activity. Then, students create their own sentences and share with the whole class. The interaction allows students to practice creating and interpreting context clues.

Who/What Am I?

Similarly, you can use guessing games to teach your students to read and write with context clues. Lindsay Yearta incorporated writing short poems with their students to reinforce context clues. In Lindsay's class, students wrote a four-line, Who Am I? poem to apply their knowledge of inventors.

Who Am I?

Who am I? I invented the phone so that I could call home. My last name rhymes with cell. Are you able to tell?	*Alexander G. Bell* (**Asia**)
Who are we? We invented the airplane. As the oldest, my name reminds you of a pig in *Charlotte's Web*. As the youngest, my name reminds people of a type of food. Our last name is the opposite of left.	*Wilbur and Orville Wright* (**Kole**)

Similarly, you can do What Am I? concept poems to also reinforce application of context clues.

What Am I? Poems

A person, a place, or a thing;
a dance, a mall, a song that you sing;
a teacher, a store, a brand worn with flair;
I can be found most anywhere!
noun

In every sentence you'll find me there.
I jump, I run, I bend, and I share.
I am, I was, I will always be.
When you write a sentence, don't forget me!
verb

Context Clues and Reading Aloud

One of my favorite ways to encourage the use of context clues during whole group reading is Finish the Sentence. This is a popular activity during my workshops, using the book *Testing Miss Malarkey*. I go through the text and choose several phrases that are unique and make sense in context. Usually, it's the last half of a sentence. I put these on large cards and distribute the various phrases to small groups. After giving them time to read their phrase and discuss how the sentence might start, I begin the story. I explain to them that I will periodically stop, which means someone else needs to finish the sentence using their cards. Students can either pick a spokesperson to read it aloud, or they can read it together as a group. Not only do students have to actively listen for the best context for their phrase, I also intersperse questions to everyone about what we are reading so everyone understands how to make contextual connections.

Recognizing words is one of those skills we take for granted if we are good readers, but it is foundational for success. And don't forget the most important strategy: teaching students to ask themselves, "Does this make sense?"

Summary

- It is important to teach students to go beyond mere recitation of words.
- Teaching students effective strategies for unlocking the meaning of unknown words improves independence and comprehension.
- Young readers need to learn to recognize commonalities in words.
- Students need multiple, frequent opportunities to work with context clues to make predictions, inferences, or to monitor comprehension.

If You Would Like More Information . . .

Literature-based Mini-Lessons to Teach Decoding and Word Recognition: Grades 1–3 by Susan Lunsford, Scholastic.

Unlocking Literacy: Effective Decoding and Spelling Instruction by Marcia K. Henry, Paul H. Brookes Publishing Co.

Word Recognition Activities: Patterns and Strategies for Developing Fluency by Barbara Fox, Prentice Hall.

This site contains information on word recognition skills and strategies: http://www.eduplace.com/rdg/res/teach/rec.html/.

This site contains a lesson plan on teaching word recognition using nursery rhymes: http://www.readwritethink.org/ lessons/lesson_view.asp?id=21/.

5

See Me

Children have more need of models than of critics.

Carolyn Coats

When I was teaching, I didn't realize how much my students watched me. Every morning, I bought a newspaper and brought it to school with me. One day, I was running late, so I didn't stop to buy a paper. All day, my students asked if something was wrong. They wanted to know where my newspaper was. That day I understood that, for some of them, I was the only person they saw read a newspaper. And for all of them, I was a role model, whether I wanted to be or not!

In this chapter, we'll talk about two types of modeling. First, we'll deal briefly with the notion of role models in literacy. Then, we'll turn our attention to how we, as teachers, can use modeling as a part of our instruction.

Role Models

As I visit schools, I see a variety of posters displayed on walls. My favorite ones fall into two categories. There are posters of popular celebrities accompanied by comments about reading or learning. It's important to have those role models, since students connect and pay attention to someone they idolize. But I also like posters of what I call real people: posters of students describing their favorite books or a photo gallery of parents or people in the community with a quote about the importance of reading and writing. I was reminded of the importance of this in a visit to Coulwood Middle School. The two bulletin boards in the main hallway highlighted the importance of real reading. In addition to a board with students' comments about books, they had a *Books I'm Thankful For* board, full of titles and descriptions of those books. These are visible reminders that anyone—and everyone—can be a reader or a writer.

Whenever we had a guest speaker in class, regardless of the topic, I asked them to address how they used reading and writing in their jobs. Again, I wanted to reinforce for each of my students that literacy was a key skill needed to be successful in life and the workplace.

Modeling for Instruction

It's just as important for us, as teachers, to provide a living, daily model for our students. Tracy Smith, a former language arts teacher, points out the need to show students what we expect them to do:

> What [my students] really needed from me was a model. So, I sat in a student desk and did what I wanted the students to do. On the first day, it was a little rocky. They came in socializing like normal adolescents. Then, they would notice me and start asking, "What is she doing?" Someone inevitably would say, "Oh, she's writing in her journal. That's what we're supposed to do when we come into this class." Or "She's reading a book. I think we're supposed to get our books and begin reading." After a day or two, it became routine.

Kendra Alston is more formal in her modeling instruction. She holds Watch What I Do days. On one of those days, she picks a specific skill and models it throughout the lesson. Her students take notes on what she does, completing the left-hand column of the chart. Then, they complete the right-hand column, thinking about how they can do the same thing. The next day is You Do It Too, when students apply what they learned by doing it themselves.

Watch What I Do . . . Then You Do It Too!

What Did I Do?	What Will You Do?

Jessica Chastain uses modeling to prepare students for their first student-led portfolio assessment conferences:

> I taped a sample interview to give the students a good idea of what to expect. When the class viewed the sample interview I would stop the video after each interview question, have the students repeat each question to me and then they would write it down. The second time through we watched the whole interview with no interruptions. Then we discussed it. When I interviewed the students throughout the next week, they were prepared to share their work with me, offer me their opinions of their strengths and weaknesses, and we were able to set a goal for the next part of the year.

Because she knew this was challenging for her students, she modeled the entire process for them, and then provided scaffolded instruction to ensure their success.

Thinking Aloud

Think-Alouds are a critical part of every teacher's repertoire. When you think aloud, you're simply verbally explaining what you are thinking. Many students simply have no idea of the processes used when learning new information. They see learning as the code that is unbreakable because they don't have the key. What we know as teachers is that there are multiple steps that go into any learning process and that one way to break that down for our students is by modeling our thinking.

Amy Williams describes how she thinks aloud for her students.

> In reading, I use statements like, "I'm not sure I understood this word. But, the author is writing about _____, and the sentence right after says _____, so it must mean _____." or "When I first read this I thought that _____, but then I realized that _____ because _____."

When she teaches writing, she models her thinking during the revision process. "I showed students several drafts of a letter that I had written. We discussed the elements that changed, etc., and I walked them through my thought process as to why I changed/added information as I wrote."

Sometimes we assume everyone else would know how to talk through that process. Your strong students do that in their heads, but your struggling students do not understand it. That's why it's important to model your thinking for students.

Using Guide-O-Ramas

Ideally, you would have time to individually work with every student who is struggling in your classroom and guide them through the content. Unfortunately, that's not possible all the time. One alternative is to guide them in writing, using a Guide-O-Rama. You may already give your students a study guide or a set of questions to follow as they read a selection. The Guide-O-Rama intersperses a written think-aloud into the process. This is a helpful alternative for individual students to use during independent reading of books as in the sample, or for instances where you want students working through a shorter section of text on their own.

Guide-O-Rama Excerpt

Bridge to Terabithia	
Page	**Guiding Question**
5	Why did Jesse practice running every day? Is there a sport that you are particularly good at?
35	Can you believe that Leslie doesn't have a TV? What would you do to relax if you did not have a TV?
68	Why does Jesse not like Leslie spending time with Bill?
101	What makes Jesse's day "The Perfect Day?" What is your idea of a perfect day?
128	Where does Katherine Paterson get the title, Bridge to Terabithia? What significance does the bridge have?

Peer Modeling

Finally, don't forget that your students are models for each other. Carie Hucks uses an interactive reading strategy to build independence. "They read a passage with a partner. Every couple of paragraphs, they stop and say something. They can ask a question about the text, clarify something, make a comment, make a prediction, or make an inference. They switch each time." Notice how the activity also provides an opportunity for students to model reading, writing, and thinking for each other.

Modeling doesn't have to be hard; just think about what you do, and be intentional about showing that to your students. And don't forget, modeling isn't an option—you model for your students every day. The choice is to decide what you want to model for them.

Summary

- It is important for students to see how literacy affects the lives of their role models.
- As teachers, we are the primary models in our classroom. Students watch us to see good literacy habits.
- Use Think-Alouds or Guide-O-Ramas to show students your thought processes when reading a text or completing a writing task.
- Don't hesitate to use peer Think-Alouds in small groups to model the thought process.

If You Would Like More Information . . .

Improving Comprehension with Think-Aloud Strategies: Modeling What Good Readers Do by Jeffrey Wilhelm, Scholastic: Teaching Resources.

Teaching Reading With Think Aloud Lessons by Laura Robb, Scholastic: Teaching Resources.

This site contains a lesson plan for a think aloud: http://www.learningpt.org/literacy/adolescent/strategies/aloud.php/.

This site contains tips for how students are able to conduct independent think alouds: http://literacy.kent.edu/eureka/strategies/think_aloud.pdf/.

$\mathcal{T}$

Thinking
About Thinking

Thinking is the hardest work there is, which is probably the reason why so few engage in it.

Henry Ford

Think About It

If you could see inside your students' brains, what would you find?

One of the key strategies good readers and writers use is metacognition, which is the "act of monitoring one's unfolding comprehension of text" (Reutzel & Cooter, 2005, p. 129). To put it in simpler terms, metacognition is when your students think about their thinking! Some of my students struggled with this. They seemed to not know how to pay attention to their own thinking, which meant they weren't really connecting with the text. Sometimes they didn't even realize that they didn't understand what they were doing!

I was in a third-grade classroom and watched a lesson where the students learned to Click and Clunk. The teacher explained that reading is like a car. As long as you are clicking along, that's fine, but if you start clunking, you need to stop and fix the problem. When I was teaching, we lived near a river, and a popular activity for students was tubing. They would float down the river in an inner tube, but they needed to watch out that they didn't bump into too many rocks! That's how I explained metacognition: Think about your ride down the river through text; if you hit a bump, you have two choices. You can ignore it if it is a small rock, but if it's too big, stop and fix it so you can keep moving.

Fix It (or Fix Up) Strategies

The next step is to teach students specific Fix It strategies, which are also called Fix Up Strategies. We've talked about most of these in other chapters, but it's important to clarify these for your students as specific things they can do when they hit a bump.

Sample Fix It/Up Strategies

Adapted from *I Read It But I Don't Get It* by Chris Tovani (2000)

- Make connections to other texts, yourself, or the world.
- Stop and think about what you have read so far.
- Ask yourself a question and try to answer it.
- Paint a picture in your head of what you are reading.
- Go back and read it again.
- Go back and retell what you have read in your own words.
- Make a prediction.
- Slow down . . . or speed up.

Activities that Focus on Thinking

Thought Bubbles

One of my favorite ways to help students think about thinking is through the use of thought bubbles. As they plan their writing, they use thought bubbles to describe what different characters are thinking. Then, when they write a first draft, it's easier to include the thoughts of each character because they have specifically planned for that. You could also use thought bubbles to describe the thoughts for each side of an issue or debate.

Word Prompts

Kendra Alston discovered that she could encourage her students to think at higher levels by minimizing her prompts for writing. She turned to Focused Freewrites instead of a writing prompt:

> I give them a title but it's not too structured, just a word....With a word you can go anywhere, but with a prompt, they tend to write what "I" want. They are less likely to do that with a word. As an example, I give them the word embarrassed. That could be about you or someone else and I get more from them than "tell about a day you were embarrassed."

Similarly, at the end of a lesson, she sets up graffiti boards for reflection. She posts chart paper around the room, using different colors for each small group. At the end of the day, the students' "ticket out of the door" is to write words, phrases, or pictures about the day's topic on their poster. The posters then serve as a discussion starter for next day. As students enter the room, they "read the room" by visiting each poster to see the responses, which are then the basis for a quick review of the prior day's lesson.

Say Something Silently

Similarly, Joya Holmes uses Say Something Silently to foster student discussion in a nonthreatening way:

> I begin by teaching my students multiple ways to respond to text-predicting, questioning, clarifying, connecting, etc. Then I write on about seven to eight pieces of chart paper something significant from the text that I want them to respond to. I write in very broad terms one topic on each piece of chart paper and the students move with their small groups from topic to topic writing all over the chart paper. They can share an original thought or comment on/question a classmate's comments. I have had some of the best conversations with my students "silently"; I think they appreciate the non-threatening yet thought-provoking aspect of the activity. It also allows me to go back and reflect on what my students are thinking and most importantly, how my students are thinking.

Thinking Hats

Another way to help students think about a topic from a variety of perspectives is through the use of Thinking Hats (deBono, 1999). The process provides six different ways of viewing or discussing information and is helpful anytime you want students to look at something through different lenses.

Thinking Hats

The White Hat calls for information known or needed. "The facts, just the facts."

The Yellow Hat symbolizes brightness and optimism. Under this hat you explore the positives and probe for value and benefit.

The Black Hat is judgment—the devil's advocate or why something may not work. Spot the difficulties and dangers— where things might go wrong. Probably the most powerful and useful of the hats but a problem if overused.

The Red Hat signifies feelings, hunches and intuition. When using this hat you can express emotions and feelings and share fears, likes, dislikes, loves, and hates.

The Green Hat focuses on creativity—the possibilities, alternatives, and new ideas. It's an opportunity to express new concepts and new perceptions.

The Blue Hat is used to manage the thinking process. It's the control mechanism that ensures the Six Thinking Hats® guidelines are observed.

Source: http://www.debonogroup.com/6hats.htm

Kendra Alston uses Thinking Hats to help in the brainstorming process of argumentative (problem/solution) writing. "The students had to think of a problem and used the Thinking Hats strategy as a way to help them elaborate/support and as a way to organize their essays. We also used it in Class Meeting as a type of conflict resolution strategy." You could also use Thinking Hats in debates to connect thinking and speaking.

Any of these activities can be easily adapted for students at almost any grade level. And they can be used for reading, writing, listening, or speaking. After all, isn't thinking the foundation for all areas of literacy?

Summary

- Teaching students to monitor their understanding also means teaching them to recognize when they start to struggle.

- Fix It strategies can help students when they hit a bump in their comprehension.

- You can integrate countless activities to help students focus on their thinking. Frequent, routine use of such strategies strengthens your students' abilities to independently comprehend a text or new idea.

If You Would Like More Information . . .

I Read It, but I Don't Get It: Comprehension Strategies for Adolescent Readers by Cris Tovani, Stenhouse Publishers.

Six Thinking Hats by Edward de Bono, Penguin Books Ltd.

This site contains thinking strategies for students: http://www.bayvieweduc.ednet.ns.ca/Smoran/Reader'sworkshop/fix_up_strategies.htm/.

This site contains metacognitive strategies: http://www.nwlincs.org/mtlincs/pilotproject/studyskills/ss1.pdf/.

U

Up or Down?

At the table in the kitchen, there were three bowls of porridge. Goldilocks was hungry. She tasted the porridge from the first bowl. "This porridge is too hot!" she exclaimed. So, she tasted the porridge from the second bowl. "This porridge is too cold," she said. So, she tasted the last bowl of porridge. "Ahhh, this porridge is just right," she said happily and she ate it all up.

Goldilocks and the Three Bears

Think About It

Do some of your students read books that are too easy for them? Do others find that books are too hard? What is just right?

After one of my presentations, a teacher stopped me and asked, "Does the level of a book really matter? As long as my students are reading, isn't that all that counts?" I don't believe it is quite that simple. I agree that we want students to read, and any reading is better than no reading, but it is important to think about how we can help our students select books.

The Reading Process

There are a variety of factors to consider when thinking about how readers interact with text. Let's think about it like a triangle.

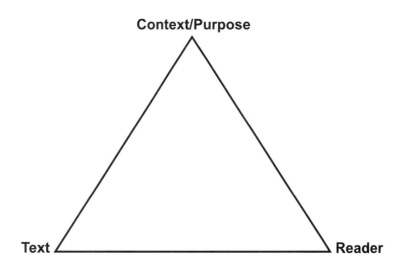

Context

The first point on the triangle is the context or purpose of the reading experience. Why is the student reading? Is he or she choosing a book to read for fun? Are you selecting a book to read aloud to your class? Is this an article your class is reading to gain information? Think of it this way: when you go to the beach for vacation, you probably don't take a research textbook with you to read. You might if you are in graduate school, but even then, that's not for fun! Your choice is probably some type of popular fiction, which is written at an easier level, usually around sixth grade. There is a reason books are called popular fiction; part of their popularity is that they flow easily and you can simply immerse yourself in the story and enjoy the experience.

Conversely, when you do need to read text at a more difficult level, such as memos, technical testing data, or the latest legislation that mandates something you are to do in your classroom, you can read that with a different focus. The same is true for students. They need opportunities to self-select text that is easy for them to comprehend, which allows them to become more fluent (see Chapter F: Fluency Builds Confidence) and more confident readers. But they also need to learn to handle more challenging text, which is where your guidance and instruction help.

Reader-Based Characteristics

As readers, your students bring their own characteristics to each reading experience. These include their interests and their life experiences to help them connect with the text. They also have prior knowledge about the topic and their prior experiences with reading. If they have felt successful before, they are more confident approaching new text. If they struggled in the past, they are less confident. Finally, some of your students are at different developmental and ability levels, which impacts text selection. For example, an older student who is reading far below grade level may be embarrassed to read books about bunnies and kittens. However, a younger reader who is reading far above grade level might be able to read a book with content that is too adult for them.

Text Materials

There are three aspects to the text to consider. First is the readability level, which is simply how hard or easy the words are to read and understand. You've probably seen readability levels on books; most publishers identify a level. This might be a grade equivalency, such as 4.5, meaning fourth grade, fifth month, or it might be a number or level determined by the publisher. Usually these levels are based on some type of formula that considers the number of syllables in words, the length of sentences, or a ranking of word frequencies.

The text support features in a book or article are also important. These features include items such as subheadings, pictures or charts, or highlighting of new words. Good text support can make a challenging text easier. Just think of textbooks and how many features are built in to help students understand the material. Lack of text support can make easy text more difficult. I remember when my neighbor's daughter, Maggie, wanted to borrow one of my *Magic School Bus* books. She was four, and loved to read, but she hated the *Magic School Bus*. They are great books, but can be confusing for emerging readers. The additional text that is part of the pictures can be distracting, and, for a beginning reader who is still learning to understand the main text, it's a challenge.

A final consideration about the text is what I like to think of as the flavor. Sometimes, we choose a book simply because of the overall quality, because of the author's style, or because it is a classic book. This can be subjective, but it is no less important. In other words, sometimes you or your students will choose to read something just because you think it is good!

Most Popular Readability Formulas

Name of Formula	Brief Description	Helpful Web Sites
Fry	The most widely used of the readability formulas. The Fry is based on the assumption that the longer the sentence and the longer the word, the more difficult the passage.	http://users.marshall.edu/~jrdeal/frygraph-bw.pdf
Flesch-Kincaid	The Flesch-Kincaid is embedded in Microsoft Word programs and checks documents for the reading level of the passage.	http://csep.psyc.memhis.edu/cohmetrix/readabilityresearch.htm
The Lexile Framework	The Lexile Framework is a computerized formula that analyzes entire text selections by sentence length and word frequency. It allows you to link difficulty of text materials with standardized tests. The web site provides a searchable database of books, and many national and state tests also provide Lexile levels for students based on the test scores.	http://www.lexile.com
Fountas and Pinnell Benchmark Assessment System	There are nine levels in the Fountas and Pinnell System. A thorough description of each of the levels (A through I) can be found on page 5 on the document located on the cirera.org web site.	http://www.fountasandpinnellleveledbooks.com/ http://www.ciera.org/library/reports/inquiry-1/1-010/1-010.pdf

Making the Right Choice for Instruction

Understanding these areas and how they interact can help us make good choices for texts in our classroom. For example, I was observing a student teacher who was reading a book aloud to her second graders. It was evident, as she asked a series of questions, that the students were familiar with the book and had read it many times before. If she had been revisiting the book to teach sequence or was using choral reading to build fluency, it would have been appropriate, but that wasn't her lesson. She was teaching prediction, and her questions were built on the notion that her students hadn't read the book. She forgot to consider context!

When reading aloud to students, I like to choose materials that fit my purpose, such as modeling a certain type of reading or rereading for fluency. But one key purpose is for students to hear text that is written at a more difficult level than they can read on their own. This provides them with an idea of where they will be reading independently in the future. That means I should consider their ability levels and pick something harder.

Another common issue as you think about these areas is helping students select texts for assignments. Shortly, we're going to talk about self-selection for fun and fluency, but there are times you want students to have a choice within some parameters. When I assigned my students to go to the library and pick a book for a book report, it was chaos. My best readers raced to get their books first, usually picking a book with less pages and lots of pictures. Then, my struggling readers would end up with a book that was much longer and harder than they could handle. I learned to require them to find a book that was around their reading levels, so the assignment was right for them—not too easy and not too hard.

Similarly, Jane Crouse and Kaye Hollifield at the Pumpkin Center Middle School library use Lexile readability levels to help students select books, which Jane describes:

> Having the library Lexiled allows students to go to the search stations and pull up a list of the books that we have in their Lexile range. It also allows me to personalize each student's reading as I help them choose a book. Printing lists for special needs students and reluctant readers has helped them use the Lexile score more effectively as they search for that special book.

Student Self-Selection

It is also critical for your students to have opportunities to self-select books for reading. I prefer to give students latitude in book choice, providing them with lots of choices of different types of materials: books, magazines, comic books, real-life reading materials, and so on. I also recommend providing information to students so they can find books at different levels. One method I like is Four Squares, which basically means having books at four levels: easy, medium, hard, and "Let's find out!" You can use boxes or shelves for each category. The first three are self-explanatory, but the fourth is my wild card. I choose books at all the other levels, but they are books I think my students might overlook if I didn't make them special. For middle school students, I include a copy of the driver's manual. The readability is high, and if it on the hard shelf, many students won't choose it. But as a let's find out choice, it's quite popular. I also mix in comic books and some popular magazines, such as *Sports Illustrated* (the regular one and the kids' version), so students aren't intimidated by the option.

Goldilocks Rules

Lori Carter, author of the Book Nuts Reading Club web site (http://www.booknutsreadingclub.com/) has a great set of guidelines for book selection. Using the parallel to Goldilocks, she provides questions your students can ask themselves to determine if a book is too easy, too hard, or just right!

Goldilocks Rules

Too Easy Books	Just Right Books	Too Hard Books
1. Have you read this book many times before?	1. Is this book new to you?	1. Are there more than a few words on a page that you don't recognize or know the meaning of? Remember the *Five Finger Test*.
2. Do you understand the story very well without much effort?	2. Do you understand most of the book?	
3. Do you know and understand almost every word?	3. Are there a few words per page that you don't recognize or know the meaning to instantly? Remember to use the *Five Finger Test*.	2. Are you confused about what is happening in most of the book?
4. Can you read it smoothly and fluently without much practice or effort?	4. Can someone help you with the book if you hit a tough spot?	3. When you read are you struggling and does it sound choppy?
		4. Is everyone busy and unable to help you if you hit a tough spot?

Source: http://www.booknutsreadingclub.com/goldilocksrule.html

Five Finger Test

1. First choose the book you think you would like to read.

2. Find a page of text somewhere in the middle of the book. Find a page with lots of text (words) and few or no pictures.

3. Begin to read the page. It is best to read the page aloud or in a whisper if possible while doing the test so you can hear the places where you have difficulty.

4. Each time you come to a word you don't know, hold one finger up.

5. If you have all five fingers up before you get to the end of the page, wave the book goodbye. It is probably too difficult for you right now. Try it again later in the year. If you need help finding a book, ask your teacher or librarian.

Source: http://www.booknutsreadingclub.com/fivefingertest.html/

Recently, a teacher told me she reworded those labels. Her students would automatically exclude books that were labeled easy or hard, but she wanted them to understand how the purpose of reading can make a difference. Instead, she used "I Can Do This Easily By Myself," "I Can Read and Learn More," and "I Need Some Help to Read This Book." As I've said before, I recommend you think about these ideas and choose or adapt what works best for you.

Summary

- Students need to read with different purposes in mind. Teaching them to realize the context in which they are reading and providing opportunities for different types of texts enhances their literacy skills.

- Three aspects to consider when helping students choose a book to read include readability level, text support features, and author's style (in relationship to reader preferences).

- When reading for instruction in your classroom, choose texts that fit the specific purpose of your lesson, and make sure the difficulty level is just slightly above the current independent reading ability of your students.

- Frequent opportunities for self selection of texts provide student ownership as well as encourage a love for pleasure reading; however, it is important for you to give students guidelines and suggestions for choosing their own books.

If You Would Like More Information

The Fountas & Pinnell Leveled Book List, K–8, 2006–2008 Edition by Irene C. Fountas and Gay Su Pinnell, Heinemann.

Leveled Books, K–8: Matching Texts to Readers for Effective Teaching by Irene C. Fountas and Gay Su Pinnell, Heinemann.

Leveling Books K–8: Matching Readers to Text by Brenda M. Weaver, International Reading Association.

This site contains a database of leveled books: www.lexile.com/.

This site contains information on reading levels: http://www.hoagies gifted.org/reading_levels.htm/.

V

Value in Variety

Good art is art that allows you to enter it from a variety of angles and to emerge with a variety of views.

Mary Schmich

Think About It

How often do you give your students choices as to how they learn or show you they understand?

Differentiated Instruction (DI) is a popular concept, and I hear many interpretations of its meaning. For most teachers, it means creating lessons that include different elements to meet the needs of each individual student in a diverse classroom. According to the DI technical definition, a teacher varies the content (what), process (how), or product (demonstration of learning) of instruction to enhance student understanding.

One concern I hear from teachers is that differentiation means some students will miss some aspects of learning. In sports, there are basic warm-up exercises and drills that every player does. Good coaches work with each player during practice to also increase strengths and strengthen any weaknesses. During instruction, we need to do the same thing. We should teach core information to everyone and adjust our lessons based on what we know about our students to help every individual reach his or her potential.

Basics of Differentiation

There is a basic decision you need to make related to differentiation. Do you want to differentiate based on learning styles, students' interests, or their skill development? That choice may change for different lessons and is driven by how you plan to match your students' needs. Let's look at several ways to differentiate your instruction.

Differentiating Text Materials for Ability Levels

I spoke with teachers in an elementary school about differentiation of content. They had a large percentage of students working above grade level, some on grade level, and the rest were reading below grade level. Fourth grade teachers typically chose one novel for all students to read each month. One teacher explained, "I'm not sure we're really meeting anyone's needs. The books are fun, but they are too hard for a few students, and I think they are probably too easy for a good portion of my students."

The next month, instead of choosing one book, we found four books at varying readability levels on the same topic. Students were then reorganized in groups based on their ability levels to read and discuss the novels. Each teacher met with one of the four groups to facilitate discussions and ensure understanding. Then students returned to their original classrooms, and all teachers led whole-group discussions about Langston Hughes. A key element of this process was that the different books each contained some information the other groups did not read. During the class discussion, the teachers asked questions to elicit specific information from each group.

One of the benefits was that even students in the lowest reading group had specific information to contribute to the discussion, reinforcing everyone's importance to the group. Also, students who could read at a higher level were challenged to do so. Finally, students were placed into new groups, with members having read the different novels, so they could create a final project about Langston Hughes. By using flexible groupings, the teachers were able to meet their students' needs more effectively.

Langston Hughes Book List

Title	Author(s)	Lexile*
Shatter with Words: Langston Hughes	Margo Sorenson	370L
Langston Hughes: Great American Poet	Patricia and Fredrick McKissack	530L
Coming Home: From the Life of Langston Hughes	Floyd Cooper	AD770L
Langston Hughes: Young Black Poet	Montrew Dunham	860L
Langston Hughes: Poet of the Harlem Renaissance	Christine M. Hill	890L
The Political Plays of Langston Hughes	Susan Duffy and Langston Hughes	1210L
The Life of Langston Hughes	Arnold Rampersad	1290L
Langston Hughes: Folk Dramatist in the Protest Tradition, 1921–1943	Joseph McLaren	1450L

For more information on Lexiles, see Chapter U: Up or Down.

Multiple Intelligences Theory

In *Frames of Mind: The Theory of Multiple Intelligences*, Dr. Howard Gardner describes eight types of intelligence. As teachers, we can use this information to connect with students in new and increasingly effective ways.

Multiple Intelligences

Linguistic	Learns best through words/language
Logical-Mathematical	Learns best through logic and/or numbers
Spatial	Learns best through visuals or pictures
Musical	Learns best through rhythms and/or music
Intrapersonal	Learns best through self-reflection and/or individually
Bodily-Kinesthetic	Learns best through physical activity
Interpersonal	Learns best through social interaction
Naturalist	Learns best through experiences in nature

Activities for Multiple Intelligences

Once you understand the different intelligences, you can use them to create activities that enhance learning for your students. Of course, this doesn't mean that you should find out each student's type of intelligence and then only teach him or her lessons in a way that matches that intelligence. I find that to be limiting and impractical for today's classrooms. Instead, incorporating activities that address various intelligences allows students to construct deeper knowledge by seeing the concept through the different intelligence lenses. For example, I may be a linguistic learner, but my knowledge of geography is certainly enhanced through visuals (spatial). So although you may want to provide instruction individually tailored to a student's intelligence(s), also plan lessons for all students that incorporate elements of the different intelligences.

Sample Literacy Activities for Multiple Intelligences

Linguistic	Logical-Mathematical
Participate in two character debates Use dialogue in reading and writing Play word puzzle games	Create timelines of events Use Venn diagrams for comparison Play games to form words using dice with letters
Spatial	**Musical**
Draw or build settings Create posters of grammar rules Write concrete poems	Write and sing songs Associate rhythms with different characters Read and write tongue twisters
Intrapersonal	**Bodily-Kinesthetic**
Keep logs of silent reading Allow for self-assessment of strengths and challenges Read aloud to a stuffed animal	Role play story or act out spelling words Play Simon Says with word actions Make letters with clay, paint, or sand
Interpersonal	**Naturalist**
Participate in choral reading or Reader's Theatre Hold mock talk shows Share writing through the Author's Chair or an "Open Mic" night at your classroom café	Hold Read and Write Outside Days Go on a nature walk for a prewriting activity Create a natural habitat to demonstrate understanding of reading

Tic-Tac-Toe for Multiple Intelligences

A simple way to provide the different activities for your students is to create a tic-tac-toe game (see template). Simply fill in the boxes with an activity for that intelligence, and allow your students to choose how to complete the game.

Tic-Tac-Toe Board Template

Interpersonal	Naturalist	Linguistic
Musical	Choose Your Own Activity	Logical-Mathematical
Bodily-Kinesthetic	Intrapersonal	Spatial

Differentiation in Action

Dani Sullivan uses multiple intelligences with her middle school students as she teaches a class novel, *They Cage the Animals at Night*. She began by informally assessing her students and explaining the different types of intelligences. In addition to writing a reflection about their growth as a learner, students complete projects that match their intelligence strengths. What a great way to shift ownership for learning to students, while customizing instruction to meet their needs!

Differentiated Instruction Activities

Multiple Intelligences Activity Chart:
They Cage the Animals at Night Unit

1950s Station Rotation	Student Selected Project Choices
Art Class: Compare the 1950s covers with their modern day counterparts, and then explain what type of characteristics makes a hero today and how that is significant to the 1950s.	**Art Class:** Create a 1950s-style comic strip dealing with a teen issue in 2007 with a summary explaining why you did what you did.
Character Ed: Look at the images and create a list of popular stereotypes of the 1950s. What do you suppose is the typical American family? How are men and women portrayed differently? Why does the media portray them in this manner?	**Character Ed:** Analyze family stereotypes conveyed through television programs of the 1950s and compare them to their modern day counterparts. Explain how the changes in the stereotypes convey a shift in our cultural values.
Commons: The vignette provides a glimpse into the past of playing with toys. Compete to see who can hula-hoop and yo-yo the longest. Then explain why toys have changed and predict what future toys will be like.	**Commons:** Compare and contrast the look, use, materials, and popularity of 3 toys of the 1950s to today's version and speculate as to why the changes did or did not take place.
Dance and Fitness: Look through the out-line of the history of rock 'n' roll, listen to selected songs, and see who can dance the best. Consider the following: Elvis Presley was made famous by his nontraditional dancing ways; how could you take some of his ideas to create an innovative dance trend?	**Dance and Fitness:** Explain the significance of your choice and either create a dance fashioned after the 1950s or sing/play a song from the 1950s.
Home Economics and Technology: Post World War II, people of the 1950s were fascinated with gadgetry and technology. Look at some of the pictures to see some of the newest technology of the time and read about how innovative the inventions were. Explain the following: how is our culture still obsessed with technology, and how does gadgetry reinforce stereotypes?	**Home Economics and Technology:** Create a presentation that compares and contrasts at least 4 pieces of technology from the 1950s to their modern day counterparts. Include an explanation as to why these changes may have occurred.

1950s Station Rotation	Student Selected Project Choices
Language Arts: Examine the slang terms and identify any that you have seen before. Explain how you think words have changed over the past 50 years and speculate about whether or not it will continue.	**Language Arts**: Create a slang dictionary of 30 terms/phrases analyzing the language used in the '50s and translate them into modern day terminology.
Picture Day: Examine some of the fashions of the 1950s in the photographs and illustrations. Consider the following: the term *teenager* was coined in the 50s. How did they go about breaking out of their shell and finding freedom for expression?	**Picture Day**: Research fashion trends of the '50s and create original clothing designs for daytime and eveningwear. Explain how and why your designs appear the way they do.
Media Class: Look at the advertisements of the 1950s and examine how the products were marketed to the consumer of the 1950s. How is the advertising different today? Explain how the media has played a role in changing cultural values.	**Media Class**: Create a commercial for 1 to 3 products from the 1950s in true '50s style. If you don't have a camera to record a commercial, create a story board of your advertisement. Include an explanation of how/why your commercial would have *spoken* to the TV audience of the time.
Social Studies: Watch the PowerPoint presentations and choose one year of interest. Record three major events that happened that year with detailed notes. Explain how those events are relevant to what is happening in today's world.	**Social Studies**: Research 1 to 3 years in the 1950s and create a news broadcast that interestingly conveys the headline news to the audience. You must include a resources page of where you got your information, and link at least one event to a current event in 2007.
Note: All learning centers were done in small collaborative groups, and not all projects were completed with partners.	

Differentiating your instruction to match the needs of your students can enhance their understanding. Let's go back to Mary Schmich's quote at the beginning of the chapter and adapt it to our purpose: "Good learning is learning that allows you to enter it from a variety of angles and to emerge with a variety of views."

Summary

- Differentiated Instruction involves variations in content, process, and product to enhance student learning.

- There are different ways to differentiate instruction: by learning style, student interest, or skill development. For a teacher, the method of differentiation is a crucial decision.

- Differentiating for multiple intelligences can draw on students' strengths, but it is also important to sometimes help them build on their weaknesses.

If You Would Like More Information . . .

The Differentiated Classroom: Responding to the Needs of all Learners by Carol Ann Tomlinson, Association for Supervision and Curriculum Development.

Differentiated Instruction for Language Arts: Instructions and Activities for the Diverse Classroom by Hannah Jones, J.W. Walch Publisher.

Differentiated Literacy Strategies for Student Growth and Achievement in Grades K–6 by Gayle Gregory, Corwin Press.

Differentiating Instruction in a Whole-Group Setting: Taking the Easy First Steps into Differentiation by B. Hollas, Crystal Springs Books.

This site contains the article, *Differentiating Reading Instruction in the Language Arts Classroom* by Janice Christy: http://www.glencoe.com/sec/teachingtoday/subject/diff_reading_la.phtml/.

W

Writing and Reading
for Real Life

When I was growing up, the Three Rs were reading, writing, and 'rithmetic. Today, in literacy, the Three Rs are reading, writing, and real life.

Barbara R. Blackburn

Think About It

How often do your students read and write using real-world materials?

When I was teaching, I fell into a common trap. I used a wide variety of stories and books in my class, but except for textbooks, I focused on reading and writing fiction. As a student, I loved reading stories that took me to a different place, so I taught those stories. But, once again, my students taught me an important lesson: I was ignoring real-life examples of reading and writing. And that meant I wasn't really meeting the needs of my students.

My first year teaching at-risk students, I asked my principal if I could teach reading using *USA Today*. At that time, *USA Today* was new, and it was the only paper to print in color. My students were excited to read "real stuff," and they were ultimately more engaged and more successful reading shorter text pieces. I also used articles in the paper to segue back to literature.

Lennie was one of my most reluctant readers. He did not see the value of reading until he turned 15 and needed to take the test to get his driver's permit. He discovered he needed to be able to study the manual to pass the test, so he asked me to teach him how to read the driver's manual. I agreed, and that evolved into some very effective lessons with all students. Online sources, magazines, newspapers, and even comic books can supplement and enhance your instruction.

Authentic Materials

Think about the text materials you teach or have in your classroom for a moment. What percentage is fiction? If it's high, I'm not suggesting you decrease that amount; I'm asking you to think about adding other real-life materials. I was attending a state meeting, and the testing coordinator told the group that the state test for reading was 60% nonfiction. The elementary teachers in the room were stunned, and several of them shared with me that they didn't teach a lot of nonfiction. They were afraid they would have to give up reading all their favorite books, but we discussed how to balance reading selection. Include your favorite stories, but mix in additional materials.

There is another way to do this. A common activity in classrooms is to read a fictional story or novel. Simply add a follow-up activity, comparing the fictional text to nonfiction information. For example, if your students read the book *The Watsons Go to Birmingham–1963* by Christopher Paul Curtis, they can make a comparison with Birmingham, Alabama, during the Civil Rights period as well as Birmingham today. Or, you could do a similar activity with *A Long Way from Chicago* by Richard Peck, comparing it to Chicago, Illinois, during the Great Depression and today. Instead of reading and discussing one story, students are required to use research skills, cite sources, and compare and contrast information from a variety of sources. The new activity requires all students to think at higher levels.

A Print-Rich Environment

In Chapter B: Building a Strong Base, I discussed the importance of providing students a print-rich environment. However, that is not limited to young children. All students need to see and have access to examples of real-life materials. Recently, I visited Chris Webb's classroom and was struck by the authentic text materials displayed on his walls. He had movie posters, charts, graphs, maps, and two large newspaper articles. The first one was a set of countdown facts about the most recent Stanley Cup Champions, and the second was an article about respect and the National Basketball Association Championship team. Having items like that posted in your room sends a message to your students that real-life reading is important.

Examples of Real Life Text Materials for Reading and Writing

- Comic books
- Magazines
- Song lyrics
- Driver's manual
- Catalogs
- College brochures and application materials
- Job applications and manuals
- E-zines (online magazines)
- Blogs
- Reference materials (dictionary, thesaurus, etc.)

Note: Be sure to find age-appropriate versions of suggestions.

Writing for Authentic Purposes

Just as students are more motivated to read for authentic purposes, they prefer writing for authentic purposes. Think of your students right now. Would they rather write a paragraph or a commercial? Would they prefer a poem or a theme song? *USA Today* regularly profiles teachers through their All-USA Teacher Team. Mark Mueller, a member of the 2004 team, notes, "I'm interested in all forms of communication—essays, scripts, stories, plays, web sites, debates, advertising. The underlying skill is the ability to express ideas well. Writing, communication, and logical thought are the keys to opening up their future." Through authentic writing, students learn to prepare for the future.

RAFT Strategy

Perhaps you would like your students to write a paragraph about a topic you have been teaching in class. We can show students real life applications using the RAFT strategy (Santa, Havens, & Macumber, 1996). RAFT stands for Role/Audience/Format/Topic. Using this strategy, students assume a role, such as an astronaut, and write from that perspective to a more authentic audience, such as people reading his online blog. In this case, students are required to understand the topic at a higher level to complete the task.

RAFT Examples

Role	Audience	Format	Topic
Lawyer	Jury	Closing argument	The wolf is innocent (The Three Little Pigs)
Hannah Montana	Lily	Text message	Weekend plans
Travel agent	Potential customers	Brochure	Encouraging visit to city or state
Newspaper reporter	Readers	Obituary	Describing historical person
Graphic artist	Public	Editorial cartoon	Water use in the middle of a drought

Technology for Literacy

Dani Sullivan incorporates technology to spark interest from her tech-savvy students. As she explains, "I use Radio Dramas and iPodcasts, have my students create Character Masquerade Blogs, write e-books, and use a GPS (global positioning system) for Literary Elements Scavenger Hunts." That sounds high-tech to me, but her students were enthusiastic as they described to me all the things they learn in her class.

Also, technology isn't just for older students. Connie Forrester provides examples for younger students below.

Technology for Younger Students

- Take digital photographs of local stores, restaurants, and places of interest (these can be used to connect print to real life).
- Take digital photographs of a classroom activity (print these and use for sequencing activity).
- Have groups of students create PowerPoint presentations as a project after a unit of study with the help of parent volunteers.

The lesson I learned from these teachers was simple; use whatever technology you have available to help your students be creative!

As I was writing this chapter, I remembered a question from my first job interview. I interviewed with a principal to take over in the middle of the school year. He asked me this question: "You come into your classroom, and there has been a mix-up. The custodian has cleared all materials out of your room. All you have is a Sears Catalog. Tell me how you would teach all subjects for the day with only that." WOW! I had to think fast! I must have answered appropriately because I was hired. I still remember what a fantastic question that was. More importantly, as I think about that today, I realize how insightful he was. Students learn best when they can see the value in learning, and how better to do that than with real-life materials and examples?

Summary

- Using authentic materials to teach literacy skills in your classroom may mean you need to find more real-world, informational text materials.
- Newspapers can be an excellent source to make reading and writing real for students.
- Students can be given opportunities to write from various perspectives in a wide range of formats using RAFT.
- Technology is one avenue to channel student interest in reading and writing in today's society.

If You Would Like More Information . . .

Early Years Non-Fiction: A Guide to Helping Young Researchers Use Information Texts by Margare Mallett, RoutledgeFalmer.

Making Nonfiction and Other Informational Texts Come Alive by Kathy Pike and Jean Mumper, Allyn and Bacon.

Nonfiction Matters: Reading, Writing, and Research in Grades 3–8 by Stephanie Harvey, Stenhouse Publishers.

Real-Life Writing Activities for Grades 4–9 by Cherlyn Sunflower, Jossey-Bass.

Reading & Writing Informational Text in the Primary Grades: Research-Based Practices by Nell K. Duke and V. Sus Bennett-Armistead, Scholastic: Teaching Resources.

Teaching Students to Read Nonfiction: Grades 4 and Up by Alice Boynton and Wiley Blevins, Scholastic: Teaching Resources.

This site contains information on opportunities for students to have writing published: www.ncte.org/.

X Factor

Extend a hand whether or not you know it shall be grasped.

Ryunosuke Satoro

Think About It

How do you view parents and families of your students? As those who can support your role as the teacher? As partners? Or in a different way?

As you build an environment that encourages literacy, a key supporting factor is how you partner with the parents and families of each of your students. Let's look at how you can REACH out to them.

REACH

R	Relationship building
E	Enrichment activities
A	Asking for help
C	Communication
H	Homework

Relationship Building

One of the lessons I learned from my students was the importance of building a relationship with their parents and other family members. To help your students be successful, the support of their parents is key. And it's up to us to take the first step.

I called every parent or a family member during the first month of school to introduce myself and tell them something positive about their son or daughter. I thought of parent relationships like a bank: I needed to make a deposit before I made a withdrawal. I didn't want my first phone call to be the one about Ashley making a poor grade or being a discipline problem.

I remember it took 17 calls to reach one parent at 7 AM as she started her shift at work. It took about 5 minutes to convince her I wasn't calling because Marcus was in trouble. She finally said she had never received a call from a teacher telling her something positive about her son. She thanked me and immediately offered her help anytime I needed it. Five weeks later when Marcus was in trouble in class, she supported me 100%. It's our responsibility to connect with parents, and the benefits outweigh any costs in terms of time.

Janelle Hicks, a kindergarten teacher, builds a relationship with her students and their families prior to the start of the school year:

> My assistant and I visited all of our students before school started this year. We sent each family a letter welcoming them to our classroom and telling them that we would be "dropping in" to visit on a certain day during a 2-hour window. We asked them to please make every effort to be home. It took a lot longer than we had planned, but it was well worth the effort. Each visit lasted 5 to 10 minutes. We introduced ourselves, met the child and any family members. We gave each child a book and a memo that had important "Beginning of the Year" school dates. We also spent a few minutes answering any questions that the children or parents had. I will never NOT do that again! It was so powerful in connecting with families at the beginning of the year and making that initial positive contact. I felt that my families were on board right away with what we were going to do in Kindergarten this year. Giving students books immediately showed them that reading was going to be important this year and put books in homes where there may not be an abundance of reading material.

I spoke with a principal in a school where there were some situations that were quite challenging. In those cases, the principal or the school resource officer (out of uniform) would accompany the teachers. It's also important to accommodate the family members' needs as much as possible. Provide lots of options for the timing and location. You may have families who prefer to meet you at McDonald's or the library. Help them feel comfortable about meeting you and you'll accomplish more.

If home visits are simply impractical for you, you can connect with students and families through writing. When Vernisa Bodison was an assistant principal at a middle school, she wrote personal letters to all incoming sixth graders. Many students wrote back, and at the start of the year, they were excited to meet their new administrator.

Enrichment Activities

I enjoyed being creative with activities that could be done at home to support literacy instruction. Although important, these activities are not required; they are ways to enrich what you are doing in the classroom. Several years ago, I met a first-grade teacher who used lunch boxes to provide at-home activities for her students. She bought lunch boxes at yard sales, and created take-home lessons. She filled each lunch box with a book, an activity card with two or three simple activities to reinforce literacy, and all the needed supplies for the activities. Students rotated taking a lunch box home for the weekend. Parents appreciate having structured opportunities to help their children at home.

Many of my reading graduate students use weekly or monthly literacy calendars, such as the one on the next page. The calendars can be posted on the refrigerator at home and include easy activities families can do together.

Parent Calendar

February

Sunday	Monday	Tuesday	Wednesday	Thursday	Friday	Saturday
Remind your child to select a book at the school library tomorrow or take your child to the public library to select a book.	Read the book with your child.	Have your child read the book to you.	Ask your child questions about the character(s) in the story. Who are the characters? What do they look like? What are some character traits? (Is the character mean, kind, honest, etc.?)	Ask your child questions about the setting of the book. Is the setting mostly outside or inside? Is the setting in a specific location? Describe the setting.	Have your child choose a word in the story that he or she did not know before. What does the word mean? How is it used in the story? Can you think of an additional way to use the same word?	Have your child read the book to a sibling or a friend.

Asking for Help

It's also important to have an attitude of asking for help. I find that, as a teacher, I can fall into the trap of telling people what to do rather than inviting them to help. That small shift can make a difference.

I try not to assume that everyone knows what to do. I was reminded of that recently when my sister called. My nephew had just started first grade and was struggling a bit with spelling words. She needed some advice on how to help him succeed. I gave her a quick list of things she could do. Providing a simple list of hints can help parents feel more successful.

Tips for Parents

- Provide a space for your child to do his/her homework.
- Set a regular time for homework.
- Be sure your child has the right tools (pencil, paper, lamp).
- Keep in regular contact with the teacher. Don't be afraid to ask questions.
- Read with your child on a daily basis.
- Visit the library with your child on the weekends. Make it a family event. Have a basket for incoming/outgoing books.
- Ensure that your child sees you reading on a regular basis.
- Have your own set time for homework each day. During this time, check to see what the teacher has sent home for you to sign or review. Also, ask your child what he or she did at school. Ask, "What did you read today? What did you make? What did you learn?"

You may also want to provide opportunities for parents and other family members to help support the literacy activities in your classroom. Many schools have set procedures for volunteers, but I always like to have a variety of choices for those who want to be more involved. Regular options can include scheduling time to be a guest reader during read-aloud time, writing down stories that young children dictate, or helping with reading and writing centers. I talked with one parent who wanted to help but could not come to school during the day because of her work hours. After talking with the teacher, she created recorded books for the classroom. She was able to do the recording at home at her convenience, and the teacher was excited to have customized tapes for her students.

Communication

In addition to building relationships at the start of the year, it's important to communicate with families throughout the year. Kendra Alston sends an interactive newsletter home every 2 weeks. It includes a question for parents to answer and send back. She has a high return rate because students receive points for returning the newsletter. Newsletters can be informational, or you could increase the literacy focus by including samples of students' writing. Older students can create their own class newsletters.

Amy Williams builds a web site for parents, which includes instructional information, simple tips for helping students, and links to other resources. I was in an elementary school where teachers had created grade-level, subject-specific bookmarks for parents that explained the state standards. Teachers simplified the information and avoided educational jargon to create a useful tool for students and parents. I've found that parents appreciate it when you provide information and tips if you do it in a way that is a bit more family friendly.

Homework

Homework can help support your literacy instruction, but it's important to be selective in the assignments. A friend of mine, Terri, explained to me that at her daughters' school the principal says the school has a no-homework policy, but "they expect students to read every day, which is life work."

When I was teaching, I tried to limit the amount of homework I assigned and to make the homework I did assign relevant. For example, I would ask students to interview a family member using a set of questions. We would then use their notes for a writing assignment. I also made sure the assignment was more creative, rather than additional practice, which enhanced the likelihood they would complete it.

Kendra Alston uses interactive homework:

> For example, I'll take a picture of something my students did in school. Then, I write "ask me what I learned today" at the top of the page. The parents have to write what their son or daughter said. This lets me know if the students even remember what happened.

As you plan your year, don't feel like you have to try all these suggestions at once. But I'd encourage you to try something. They may not work with every parent, but as Ryunosuke Satoro reminds us in the opening quote, extend your hand, regardless of whether or not anyone accepts it.

Summary

- Form a trusting relationship with your students' parents to have maximum success in your literacy classroom.

- Provide opportunities for parents to interact with their child in literacy activities.

- Parents can be a valuable resource in your literacy classroom. Don't be afraid to ask them for help.

- Share your classroom literacy goals with your parents. They are more likely to reinforce your efforts at home if they know what's going on in your classroom.

If You Would Like More Information...

Bridging School and Home Through Family Nights: Ready-to-Use Plans for Grades K–8 by Diane W. Kyle, Ellen McIntyre, Karen B. Miller, and Gayle H. Moore, Corwin Press.

Building a Culture of Literacy: Month-by-Month by Hilarie Davis, Eye On Education.

Family Literacy Connections in Schools and Communities edited by Lesley Mandel Morrow, International Reading Association.

Family Reading Night by Darcy J. Hutchins, Marsha D. Greenfeld, and Joyce L. Epstein, Eye On Education.

This site contains a lesson plan about involving families in literacy: http://www.readwritethink.org/lessons/lesson_view.asp?id=38/.

Classroom Motivation from A to Z by Barbara R. Blackburn, Eye On Education (see Chapter F: Form Partnerships).

Classroom Instruction from A to Z by Barbara R. Blackburn, Eye On Education (see Chapter O: Options for Successful Homework).

Your Turn

The best effect of any book is that it excites the reader to self-activity.

Thomas Carlyle

Think About It

How do you help your students become independent learners?

Helping students take ownership of their learning is important. Your students need to be independent, because one day you won't be there for them. But you can't just give your students work and leave them alone. You need to structure opportunities that allow them to take ownership and teach them how to grow. A good comparison for this approach is learning to ride a bike. I remember riding a tricycle when I was growing up. I was very good at it and felt quite confident of my abilities. At some point, I got a real bike for Christmas. My parents, in their wisdom, put training wheels on it while I learned to ride. Those extra wheels provided stability and balance as I learned how to ride it. Then, Dad took the training wheels off. He taught me to ride without the training wheels, but he was beside me with one hand on the seat. One day, he let go of the seat and I realized I was riding by myself. I was so excited. I had learned to ride a bike, and I loved it.

Instruction for Independence

The key to developing independent learners is to teach them how. As Jill Yates says:

> As a first grade teacher, I learned early on that I had to make no assumptions in believing that my students naturally knew what was expected, how to transition, and what being accountable and responsible for good choices meant. I have come to realize that my explicit consistency and modeling are what create and sustain the strong foundational and operational understanding I seek. And, I have found this in turn creates classes that desire and choose to pursue success, confidence, and pride.

With every activity, it's important for you to model what to do, then give your students opportunities to practice at increasing levels of independence. Let's look at some ways you can incorporate those types of activities in your classroom.

Be the Author

Students must see themselves as writers. I was in a classroom in an alternative school, and the teacher commented that her students didn't believe they were writers. As I looked around the room, I noticed there were author posters on the walls, but the posters were faded and dated. Over the next week, the teacher took digital pictures of her students. They then created new author posters—of themselves! Beside their pictures, the students wrote about their favorite books and what types of writing they enjoyed. It became a visible reminder to each student that he or she was an author.

Amy Williams also believes students need to see themselves as writers:

> In writing, I strive to make them feel that they are the author. We talk about how we always feel the author knows what is best for his/her story. When they see themselves as an author, they have more confidence in their own writing and begin to be more independent writers.

Literacy Contracts

Kendra Alston uses Literacy Contracts to help her students work independently. Both students and parents must sign the contract. Students can then complete the items in any order. She points out, "This teaches time management and allows the personality of the child to come in."

Sample Items for Literacy Contract

Poetry:	• Read poem (sample provided). • Underline similes. • Circle dialogue. • Create your own poem following the same format.
Biography:	• Read *The Story of Levis* by Michael Burgan. • Make a timeline showing major events in the story. • Show historical events in one color and events in the life of Levi Strauss in another.
Tall Tale:	• Read a tall tale. • Create a chart listing all the cause and effect relationships (three columns: cause, effect, and signal words).
Test-Taking Skill Games:	• Mom Goes on Strike (drawing conclusions). • The Last Day (sequencing). • A Delicious Mistake (author's purpose).

Be the Expert

Another way Kendra helps her students become independent is to use the Be the Expert game. With a partner, students read a section of text. Next, each student assumes a role. One student is the expert and the other is the amateur. Kendra tells them, "Pretend like you don't know; what questions would you ask?" The amateur student asks questions and the expert gives answers about the topic. She picks the expert initially, but after each section of text, the students switch roles. Students also log questions and answers, which provides an informal assessment.

Be the Expert

Amateur (question)	
Expert (answer)	
Amateur (question)	
Expert (answer)	

Book Chats

Terri Twist, remediation specialist at New Hope Elementary School, uses small-group Book Chats to help at-risk students become more independent readers:

> The students and I met one day each week a different grade level each time, with separate groups for girls and boys. The group of students came to my room during their lunch time. We started by talking about whatever was new with everyone as we ate our lunch together. We talked for about ten minutes before we started our reading. It is amazing how much you can learn about children when they are in a small, relaxed environment. Some of these students hate to read; however, most of them began reading more often on their own. The program was designed to teach students that reading can be fun. The students and I explored many types of genres and literature. Each Book Chat lasted about 45 minutes. All of the students took turns washing the table, sweeping the floor, and taking out the trash. I wanted them to have some responsibilities. I am happy to report that the students really enjoyed Book Chat. They felt that it helped them to become better readers, and all said that they would sign up again.

Reflections

Another way to help your students become independent is through the use of written reflections. I regularly ask students to take a minute to write down what they learned and, more importantly, how they know they understand the content. I want to make sure they do more than just write down a few facts; I want them to understand *why* they understand! You can do this at the end of a learning activity or you can have them write something more formal. Kendra tracks growth in her middle school students through the use of End-of-Quarter Reflections.

End-of-Quarter Reflections

For your End of Quarter essay, you will present an argument about what you have learned as a writer/reader, drawing from examples you have experienced in class. This essay is a reflective self-assessment that will involve you in reviewing all of the work you have done so that you can discuss what you've learned about reading, writing, and thinking critically.

As you begin thinking about this essay, which should be from one to two pages in length, you may respond to these questions:

- What have I learned? What have I learned that's important? How will it help me academically, personally, and/or professionally?

- What contributed to my learning? What particular assignments, techniques, and/or activities really helped? How can I demonstrate this? What evidence from class (daybook, freewriting, shared reading, etc.) can I use to support my learning?

- Why are these things important to me? What will I be able to do as a result of this learning, either as a student or as a professional, once I graduate?

- How have I developed as a writer, as a student? What specific skills, techniques, and strategies have I learned that will help? What are my strengths as a writer? What do I do well? What are my weaknesses? What do I still need to work on; what skills do I still need to develop as a reader and/or a writer?

Remember it is **my** task to evaluate you and your work. **Your** job is to reflect on your growth and development as a reader and writer.

A Final Thought

Janelle Hicks builds a strong foundation for independence with her kindergarten students:

> I do a lot during reading and writing workshops. I model for the students but then encourage them to "try it out." During writing, I will praise those students who try something new and invite them to share their writing with the rest of the class. As the chil-

dren develop reading strategies and have the opportunity to practice them during independent reading, I find that this helps them to become independent readers and writers.

That's the way to help your students succeed. Show them how, then let them try!

Summary

- Although the long-term goal is for all students to become independent learners, gradual release must be carefully planned.
- Allowing students to take ownership of their work increases their confidence and personal desire to gain independence.
- Activities such as Literacy Contracts, Be the Expert, Books Chats, and Reflections help achieve the goal of increasing student ownership.
- Frequent opportunities for student choice are crucial when attempting to have students take charge of their own learning.
- Encourage experimentation. If your students never try anything new, they'll never experience independent success!

If You Would Like More Information . . .

The Daily Five: Fostering Literacy Independence in the Elementary Grades by Gail Boushey and Joan Moser, Stenhouse Publishers.

Independent Writing: One Teacher—Thirty-Two Needs, Topics, and Plans by M. Colleen Cruz, Heinemann.

Yellow Brick Roads: Shared and Guided Paths to Independent Reading 4–12 by Janet Allen, Stenhouse Publishers.

This site contains a lesson plan on developing the reading plans necessary to support independent reading: http://www.read writethink.org/lessons/lesson_view.asp?id=836/.

Z

Zones of Literacy

You unlock this door with the key of imagination. Beyond it is another dimension—a dimension of sound, a dimension of sight, a dimension of mind. You're moving into a land of both shadow and substance, of things and ideas. You've just crossed over into the Twilight Zone.

Rod Serling, introduction to the original *Twilight Zone*

Think About It

How does the physical layout of your room support your literacy instruction?

If I walked into your classroom, would I know that literacy is important? What students see in your room can send powerful messages. I've visited rooms that simply come alive with language, and it's clear that students are learning. I walked through one school where every classroom was filled with labels (door, closet, etc.). Each room had a bulletin board of students' writing. In many of the rooms, there were author posters of the students. The student-centered nature of the school was evident.

Recently, I visited a sixth-grade classroom. Angie Krakeel and Kelly Zorn had different zones in the room. Throughout the day, students moved from the reading zone to the technology zone, and on and on. Let's look at four critical zones for any literacy classroom.

Reading Zone

The Reading Zone includes a wide range of books and other reading materials. Think about your students and their interests. You may want to include magazines, comic books, and other real-life materials. As I mentioned earlier, my students appreciated that I kept copies of the North Carolina Driver's Manual in the room, because many of them were studying for the driving test. Organize your materials so that students can find books easily. You might sort them by level, genre, or by topic. Kendra Alston always placed her books "facing outward so students could see covers." She explained that the goal was to "make reading accessible and not scary. I want students to relax and not see reading as punishment. I always gave my book center a title, like Book Work or the Bee Lounge."

Writing Zone

A Writing Zone can be filled with all the supplies students might need throughout the writing process. I kept drawing paper, lots of crayons and markers, pencils and pens, writing paper, blank journals, dictionaries (at different levels), and blank books. If your students have created class books about a topic, those could be in this zone or the Reading Zone. You might also have an author chair and reading area for students to share their writing with others.

Word Zone

This area focuses on word study. The main component is a word wall. Word walls are popular, but I've seen some that are more effective than others. For example, I visited a kindergarten classroom where words for the year were up near the ceiling. The students couldn't even see the words, and there were so many, the students were lost. Generally, word walls should be somewhere easily accessible for your students, preferably at eye level or just a bit higher. Also, as you go throughout the year, build the wall with your students. It keeps them engaged and helps them build ownership. Kendra Alston likes to go "3-D" with her word walls. She explains, "I like interactive word walls that are three dimensional. For example, if you have a word like *simile*, students can lift the flap for an example."

Work Zone

The Work Zone is a place to display student work. You might also call this your Success Zone. However, it's important to do this so that students don't view it as a competition, in which "only the best students get their work posted." Everyone needs a fair chance to have their work on display. It's a challenge, because you want to recognize good work, but you also don't want to exclude students who may not be perfect. Christy Matkovich, one of my former graduate students, has found a terrific way to balance the two by creating a Wall of Fame. Her students choose what they want to post. It may be a test (with their grade removed) or a paper. However, if what they want to display is something they did, such as helping someone else, they write that on a paper hand representing a "pat on the back" and post it. In each case her students must explain to her why they are proud of the work. That's her only criteria. Think about it: she completely shifts the ownership to her students, which is one of the best ways to enhance student motivation.

Students should also have a choice. If they truly don't want to post their work, consider finding an alternative. Susanne Okey points out:

> I have them select their work or have input. If they choose not to have anything displayed, that's OK, but I want to figure out another way to highlight some success for that child. Some are uncomfortable about handwriting or artwork, and I don't want to force them to put out in front of the world something too personal to share. Some are such perfectionists; they are never satisfied with their work. What you don't want is for something that is intended to be positive to turn negative. That's when I turn to something that is a team effort, such as group work.

Other Zones

You can create a zone for anything you want: a Quiet Zone, a Drama/Theatre Zone, a Listening Zone, or a Technology Zone. And a zone doesn't have to be a place, if you have limited space, you can choose a block of time and make that your zone. Just remember, the purpose of a zone is to concentrate on a particular area of literacy!

Summary

- The physical environment of your classroom needs to convey the importance of literacy.
- A Reading Zone in a literacy classroom should include easy access to a wide variety of texts.
- Similarly, a Writing Zone should provide a resource center for students to use pencils, editing pens, a thesaurus, paper, and so forth.
- Vocabulary words can be effectively displayed in a Word Zone.
- Displaying student work in a Work Zone helps celebrate success.
- Don't be limited. Create your own zones to support your instruction!

If You Would Like More Information . . .

That Workshop Book: New Systems and Structures for Classrooms that Read, Write, and Think by Samantha Bennett, Heinemann.

This site contains information about and pictures from a literate classroom: http://www.prel.org/toolkit/pdf/plan/Creating%20 Literate%20Environments.pdf/.

This site contains literacy resources for all teachers (kindergarten–adult education): http://www.literacy. uconn.edu/teachers.htm/.

Classroom Instruction from A to Z by Barbara R. Blackburn, Eye On Education (see Chapter L).

References

Allen, J. (2000). *Yellow brick roads: Shared and guided paths to independent reading 4-12.* Portland, ME: Stenhouse Publishers.

Antonacci, P. A., & O'Callaghan, C. M. (2006). *A handbook for literacy: Instructional & assessment strategies, K–8.* Boston: Pearson, Education, Inc.

Beers, K. (2003). *When kids can't read, what teachers can do: A guide for teachers, 6–12.* Portsmouth, NH: Heinemann.

Blachowicz, C., & Ogle, D. (2001). *Reading comprehension: Strategies for independent learners.* New York: The Guilford Press.

Burkhardt, R. M. (2003). *Writing for real: Strategies for engaging adolescent writers.* Portland, ME: Stenhouse Publishers.

Cooper, J. D., Chard, D. J., & Kiger, N. D. (2006). *The struggling reader: Interventions that work.* New York: Scholastic Theory and Practice.

Daly, E. J., III, Chafouleas, S., & Skinner, C. H. (2005). *Interventions for reading problems: Designing and evaluating effective strategies.* New York: The Guilford Press.

Daniels, H., & Zemelman, S. (2004). *Subjects matter: Every teacher's guide to content area reading.* Portsmouth, NH: Heinemann.

DeBono, E. (1999). *Six thinking hats.* New York: Little, Brown and Company.

Diller, D. (2007). *Making the most of small groups: Differentiation for all.* Portland, ME: Stenhouse Publishers.

Dorn, L. J., & Soffos, C. (2001). *Scaffolding young writers: A writers' workshop approach.* Portland, ME: Stenhouse Publishers.

Farris, P. J., Fuhler, C. J., & Walther, M. P. (2004). *Teaching reading: A balanced approach for today's classrooms.* Boston: McGraw Hill.

Fletcher, R. (2006). *Boy writers: Reclaiming their voices.* Portland, ME: Stenhouse.

Gardner, H. (1983). *Frames of mind: The theory of multiple intelligences.* New York: Basic Books.

Gunning, T. G. (2008). *Creating literacy instruction for all students* (6th ed.). Boston: Pearson Education, Inc.

Harvey, S. (1998). *Nonfiction matters: Reading, writing, and research in grades 3–8.* Portland, ME: Stenhouse Publishers.

Harvey, S., & Goudvis, A. (2007). *Strategies that work: Teaching comprehension for understanding and engagement* (2nd ed.). Portland, ME: Stenhouse Publishers.

Herrell, A. L., & Jordan, M. (2006). *50 strategies for improving vocabulary, comprehension, and fluency: An active learning approach.* Upper Saddle River, NJ: Pearson Education, Inc.

Hollas, B. (2005). *Differentiating instruction in a whole-group setting: Taking the easy first steps into differentiation.* Peterborough, NH: Crystal Springs Books.

Jacobs, H. H. (2006). *Active literacy across the curriculum: Strategies for reading, writing, speaking, and listening.* Larchmont, NY: Eye On Education.

Johns, J. L., & Lenski, S. D. (1994). *Improving reading: Strategies & resources.* Dubuque, IA: Kendall/Hunt Publishing Company.

Johnson, P. (2006). *One child at a time: Making the most of your time with struggling readers, K–6.* Portland, ME: Stenhouse Publishers.

Krashen, S. D. (2004). *The power of reading: Insights from the research* (2nd ed.). Portsmouth, NH: Heinemann.

Marzano, R. J., Pickering, D. J., & Pollock, J. E. (2004). *Classroom instruction that works: Research-based strategies for increasing student achievement.* Upper Saddle River, NJ: Prentice Hall.

May, F. B. (2006). *Teach reading creatively: Reading and writing as communication* (7th ed.). Upper Saddle River, NJ: Pearson Education, Inc.

Mueller, S. (2005). *Everyday literacy: Environmental print activities for children 3–8.* Beltsville, MD: Gryphon House, Inc.

Noden, H. R. (1999). *Image grammar: Using grammatical structures to teach writing.* Portsmouth, NH: Heinemann.

Norton, T., & Land, B. L. J. (2004). *Literacy strategies: Recourses for beginning teachers, 1–6.* Upper Saddle River, NJ: Pearson Education, Inc.

Opitz, M. D., Ford, M. P., & Zbaracki, M. D. (2006). *Books and beyond: New ways to reach readers.* Portsmouth, NH: Heinemann.

Opitz, M. F., & Rasinski, T. V. (1998). *Good-bye round robin: 25 effective oral reading strategies.* Portsmouth, NH: Heinemann.

Owocki, G., & Goodman, Y. (2002). *Kidwatching: Documenting children's literacy development.* Portsmouth, NH: Heinemann.

Paratore, J. R., & McCormack, R. L. (Eds.). (2007). *Classroom literacy assessment: Making sense of what students know and do.* New York: The Guilford Press.

Prescott-Griffin, M. L., & Witherell, N. L. (2004). *Fluency in focus: Comprehension strategies for all young readers.* Portsmouth, NH: Heinemann.

Rasinski, T. V. (2003). *The fluent reader: Oral reading strategies for building word recognition, fluency, and comprehension.* New York: Scholastic Professional Books.

Reutzel, D. R., & Cooter, R. B., Jr. (2005). *The essentials of teaching children to read: What every teacher needs to know.* Upper Saddle River, NJ: Pearson Education, Inc.

Santa, C., Havens, L., & Macumber, E. (1996). *Creating independence through student-owned strategies.* Dubuque, IA: Kendall/Hunt.

Silver, H. F., Strong, R. W., & Perini, M. (2000). *Discovering nonfiction: 25 powerful teaching strategies, grades 2–6.* Santa Monica, CA: Canter & Associates, Inc.

Smith, J. A., & Read, S. (2005). *Early literacy instruction: A comprehensive framework for teaching reading and writing, K–3.* Upper Saddle River, NJ: Pearson Education, Inc.

Southern Regional Education Board (SREB). (2004). *Literacy across the curriculum: Setting and implementing goals for grades six through 12 (Site Development Guide No. 12).* Atlanta, GA: Author.

Tomlinson, C. A. (2001). *How to differentiate instruction in mixed-ability classrooms* (2nd ed.). Oxford, OH: Association for Supervision and Curriculum Development.

Tomlinson, C. A. (1999). *The differentiated classroom: Responding to the needs of all learners.* Oxford, OH: Association for Supervision and Curriculum Development.

Tompkins, G. E. (2005). *Literacy for the 21st century: A balanced approach* (4th ed.). Upper Saddle River, NJ: Prentice Hall.

Tovani, C. (2000). *I read it, but I don't get it: Comprehension strategies for adolescent readers.* Portland, ME: Stenhouse Publishers.

Wilhelm, J. D. (2002). *Action strategies for deepening comprehension: Role plays, text structure tableaux, talking statues, and other enrichment techniques that engage students with text.* New York: Scholastic Inc.

Wilhelm, J. D. (2004). *Reading is seeing: Learning to visualize scenes, characters, ideas, and text worlds to improve comprehension and reflective reading.* New York: Scholastic Inc.

Worthy, J., Broaddus, K., & Ivey, G. (2001). *Pathways to independence: Reading, writing, and learning in grades 3–8.* New York: The Guilford Press.

Zimmermann, S., & Hutchins, D. (2003). *7 keys to comprehension: How to help your kids read it and get it!* New York: Three Rivers Press.